"This refreshing book reveals what telling the truth, combined with the grace of God, can accomplish in bringing about the healing and restoration of two souls as well as a marriage. May we all learn to dance so well!"

Carl Green, Global Training Network

"Mike and Fi have gifted all of us with a transparent glimpse into their personal life journey with such engaging honesty and candor that their story draws us further into their lives and makes us want to pursue a deeper relationship with our spouse…This is a thoroughly enjoyable account of two people working toward wholeness in Christ in spite of the immense challenges they faced."

Stephen R. Tourville, Superintendent
PennDel Ministries Nework
Asemblies of God

"As you read the pages of this book, you will feel the pain and experience the victories of Mike and Fi Lusby. When there was no reason to stay married, their commitment to marriage was the glue that kept them together. This story will compel you to believe that ALL things are possible and that, someday, you too can dance."

Anne Beiler
Founder, Auntie Anne's Soft Pretzels

And Then We Danced

Fi Lusby
Mike Lusby

Preface

This is the story of a marriage told in two parts. Please note that under each chapter title is one of two names: Mike or Fi. The name listed denotes the perspective from which that particular chapter is being told.

This is a true story. Many of the names in this book have been changed to maintain the privacy of those individuals. Also, some identities and physical descriptions have been altered or withheld.

For everything there is a season, a time for every
  activity under heaven:
A time to be born and a time to die
A time to plant and a time to harvest
A time to kill and a time to heal
A time to tear down and a time to build up
A time to cry and a time to laugh

A time to grieve and a time to dance

Ecclesiastes 3:1-4

Table of Contents:

Dedication

Study Guide

Acknowledgments

About the Authors

To our amazing sons – Greg and Gent,
Our wonderful daughter-in-love Carla,
And our sweet little grandson, Nolan.

If we would have chosen a different path
or given up,
we would never have experienced
the joy you bring to us.

To Mom Lusby,
one of the strongest women we know.
Your love has been unwavering

Chapter One
The Unexpected Telephone Call

Fi

"Fi! Telephone!"

Who would call me at my mom's house this close to Christmas?

The sound of laughter moved in waves and echoed against the walls, an endless cycle of joy. If there's anything my family knows how to do well, it's laugh until our sides ache. It was a few days after Christmas in 1997, and about fifty of us were packed into my mother's small house. In other words - enjoyable chaos.

People moved from this room to that room with plates of food, or ran outside to play games, or lingered in the kitchen talking. The back door slid open then closed, and the cold rushed in to where we sat as some of the older cousins went out to the parking lot and started a basketball game. But there were enough people in the house – no matter how much December air pushed its way inside, the place remained warm.

1

It was one of those short afternoons that comes between Christmas and New Year's Eve, when it seems that no one is at work and everyone is biding their time before yet another year begins. It was cold, as most Pennsylvania winter days are, and the breeze made it even colder. My mom's house was surrounded on three sides by open space, mostly farmers' fields, barren and brown, or pure white when there was snow.

But I was inside, with the laughter and the warmth. We had been through a lot, my extended family, which perhaps made those moments even more precious. Most of us have worked together. Many of us shared houses at some point. There are things that only families can survive.

Then there was my husband Mike and I. Our marriage hadn't gotten off to the best start (nearly 30 years before that winter day). My wedding day was one of the unhappiest days of my life. We experienced things that could have easily destroyed our relationship: his childhood, my childhood, his pain, my pain. We were beginning to understand how fortunate we were to have made it to that day, together.

Then, somewhere off in the distance, beyond the voices and the smell of Christmas cookies, Mom's telephone rang. It was one of those old-fashioned ones with a loud, clunky ring and a twisted cord that tangled in on itself. I don't know who answered it – any of us would have. She was in her late 70s, and if we happened to be in her house when the phone rang, we answered it as if it was our own phone in our own house. But I do remember someone putting a hand over the mouthpiece and yelling back through the house:

"Fi! Telephone!"

Who would call me at my mom's house?

I made my way through the chaos, stepping over crawling babies. I dodged teenagers. I took the phone and put it up to my ear.

"Hello, this is Fi," I said, squinting in an effort to hear through the din.

It was someone I hadn't seen in years. He was about ten years older than I, and our families had spent time together when I was little. He made small talk for a few moments.

I wonder how he knew to find me here.

"Fi, I have something I need to tell you," he said, his voice suddenly serious.

"Okay."

Why does he sound that way? Did I do something?

"When you were three or four years old, a few of the other boys and I sexually abused you," he said, his voice stopping abruptly, then starting up again in a slow, sorrowful way. Even in the midst of my shock, I could tell how difficult it was for him to say what he said, to put words to something so horrifying.

"I had to call and tell you. I couldn't wait any longer. I had to tell you how sorry I am that this happened."

All around me, the same sounds of happiness and laughter continued. I leaned against the wall and closed my eyes.

Chapter Two
A Barrel of Cider and a Bag of Chips

Mike

When I was a kid, one thing was for sure: if you went to the Lusby's for a holiday dinner, you never walked away hungry. The food coming out of the kitchen during one particular Thanksgiving measured up to my expectations: mashed potatoes, green beans, gravy, and the biggest turkey my five-year-old self had ever laid eyes on. I squeezed in around the large table with my cousins, aunts, uncles, parents, grandmother and all my brothers and sisters. I'm number seven of eleven, so it was a crowded feast, with people, place settings, and elbows everywhere. You'd better get what you want, and get it fast, or it would be gone.

We lived in Chester County, Pennsylvania, which in the late 50s meant farmland. These days, Philadelphia is expanding into the eastern part of Chester, but when I was a kid, small towns like Coatesville were islands in a sea of fields. You were either a town kid, or you were a country kid — there was nothing in between. I was a country kid.

My dad sat at the head of the table, laughing and shoveling in the food. He was around six feet tall, very strong and broad-shouldered. He was a farmer, built like an ox. You certainly wouldn't think anyone would want to mess with him. Not only was he a big guy, he could fight. Even then, during that Thanksgiving, I'd be surprised if he didn't have a slightly discolored eye or an ache in his ribs from the latest fistfight.

Once, my dad and brothers spent a night on the town and got into a barroom brawl. One of the other guys smashed a beer bottle and shoved the jagged glass edges into my brother's face. His whole nose just peeled right back - it was bad. No doubt my dad would have come to his defense if he hadn't already gotten hit in the head with a bottle by someone else and ended up knocked out, lying under a table at the Speakman House.

That's where dad always went to drink. He spent hours there, especially on Thursday nights after he got paid. Sometimes he took us younger kids grocery shopping with him; then he'd swing by the bar on the way home and leave us out in the car while he drank his fill and spent the rest of his paycheck buying rounds for his buddies. For hours we sat there in the car, waiting for him to come back and take us home. I don't know what we did to pass the time — probably what most little kids do: make up games and climb over the seats.

Eventually, he would come out and take us home. Back then it wasn't as big a deal to leave your kids unattended — everyone around there knew who we were and kept an eye on us.

For a little while, on that Thanksgiving Day, our family gathering was like any other holiday celebration — the good-natured teasing, the laughing, and the eating.

5

We passed food in every direction and loaded our plates. The four-bedroom farmhouse, heated by a woodstove that also served as my mom's stovetop, was filled to bursting. But then my dad brought something out that made my little spirit sink because, even at five years old, I knew what it would lead to. What did he bring out?

A cup filled with hard cider.

Cheers and laughter and the sound of chair legs scraping the wooden floor erupted as my cousins and uncles headed to the barrel down in the basement and filled their glasses. It smelled terrible – I wondered how anyone could even drink it. They stumbled up and down the basement steps, refilling their glasses again and again. They toasted each other.

During that Thanksgiving, before things got too bad, I fell asleep on the chair watching television, my belly full of food. The cold air beat against the walls, but with the wood stove and all the people inside, the house stayed warmer than usual. The scene faded as I drifted off to sleep in my own peaceful corner. For a moment, I didn't have a worry in the world.

I woke up when someone tipped over my chair and I landed with a thump on the floor. Shocked, I scrambled out of the way on all fours, trying to regain my senses and look around. The scene inside the house had deteriorated while I slept, typical of what happened when they got drunk.

I'm not sure exactly who he fought. Punches flew through the confusion, reinforced by curses, shouts of pain and the hollow, meaty sound of knuckles on flesh. They crashed into the furniture and thudded against the walls. The windows rattled. They paused only to throw up, usually in mid-fight. Soon the room stank of vomit and sweat and hard cider.

Where was my dad, you might wonder?

He was right in the middle, giving it as much as he was taking it. Everyone was angry at each other. I'm sure by that point, no one knew why.

When my brothers and uncles and dad got drunk, they just didn't care about anything. They fought and fought. They swore to kill one another. They slipped on the vomit-coated wood floors and ended up on their backs, sometimes getting up, sometimes just lying there, deciding that they'd had enough. I don't know where my mom was or my grandma. The room was total chaos.

The sad part was that this was typical. This was a normal family event for us: get together, eat, have fun, drink, get drunk, fight until you were too tired to raise your fists, sleep it off, and then become good friends again. I was young, but it was a precursor of what was to come for the rest of my childhood.

I crept away from the chaos and into the empty half of the farmhouse. The fighting and shouting took on a distant quality, as if happening at the end of a long tunnel. I was so shy, reserved, and quiet – my siblings probably thought something was wrong with me. But deep within my introverted nature, all of this drinking and fighting made me angry, and I got to the place where I would fight kids at school for no reason. I earned a reputation for being scrappy. The anger trapped inside me constantly searched for a way out, like a wild bird inside a cage.

By the time I got to middle school, no one wanted to fight me. My brother and I made a name in our community as fighters and rebels. We ran around with our gang, causing trouble and punching anyone who stood in our way. It's what we saw, what we were taught, and it's how we ended up living, at least until one evening in August of 1968 when I asked my boss Donnie if he would take me to see a preacher.

But on that cold Thanksgiving Day around 1955, I was only five years old. I found a quiet place in the other half of the house and fell asleep.

When I was young the farmhouse felt huge, but now when I drive past I don't think it looks like anything big: just a normal two-story house with a cellar and a few barns and outbuildings. We only lived in half of it, and it was tight quarters.

When I was young, all that fighting scared the daylights out of me. I'd run out to a cornfield or hide in the barn, or if the other side of the farmhouse was unlocked and vacant, I'd go over there. Something in me felt desperate to find a safe place, a quiet place.

Recently I was at a Philadelphia Phillies game and some drunk guys started fighting. It had been a long time since I had seen grown men go after each other like that, swaying and swinging lopsided punches, and the first thing I wanted to do was get out of there. Run. Urgency filled me, almost a sense of panic, and I realized that seeing my father and brothers fight so much when I was a kid had impacted me.

But there was one time I got in the way.

It happened at maybe three in the morning. The sound of my dad revving his car outside woke me up, a sound that terrified all of us. When he came home revving his engine, we knew he was drunk and looking for a fight. One night the sound scared me so badly I jumped out of my second-story bedroom window and ran, hiding in the woods. But on this particular night, I lay there quietly in my bed and waited

I heard the front door slam, then his feet on the steps. I lay in bed, my eyes wide open. I'm sure every single one of my brothers and sisters were doing the same thing: holding their breath, trying to lie completely still, heart beating a heavy rhythm in their chests, praying to God he wouldn't come into the room.

Everything went quiet. Relief began to sink in, and I felt sleep pressing in on my eyes. Maybe everything would be okay. Maybe he had already fallen asleep.

Then I heard my mom scream.

"He's choking me! God, he's going to kill me!"

I heard scuffling sounds in their bedroom, then the sound of bare feet in the hall, running. My dad's boots thudded after her, stomping down the stairs. Before I knew what I was doing, I pushed the covers off and jumped out of bed, chasing them down the steps.

I was only seven or eight, but I wasn't going to let him hurt her again.

By the time I got downstairs, they were outside. By the time I got to the front door, he was chasing her across the yard. I ran as fast as I could, out on to the porch and at an angle through the morning, hoping to cut him off. The grass was lined with dew, and it felt cold on my feet. The crisp air smelled clean. I caught up to him, grabbed his arm, and hung on for dear life.

My weight threw him off balance, and his feet slipped on the wet grass. He hit the ground hard. I slid through the dew, but fear and adrenaline had me back up on my feet, running as fast as I could for the closest barn. I sprinted into the darkness, huddled in a back corner. My mom hid somewhere else on the property.

That's the only time I got involved.

I don't remember exactly what my dad did immediately following that tackle – if it was like all the other times, he probably went in the house to sleep it off. He probably woke up hours later and ate breakfast, completely forgetting about what had happened. Too much alcohol took away his ability to remember what he had done the night before.

He probably went back out the next night and got drunk again.

The thing is, I have good memories of my dad. We had fun times with him, and there is one thing that

9

stands out about every single one of those good times: Dad was sober. When he didn't drink, he was a great dad, a loving dad who seemed to really enjoy his wife and children. It's sad, what alcohol can do to a person.

I remember one beautiful Sunday afternoon. My mom always made a big meal for Sunday lunch, so I was feeling full and content. For some reason that day my dad wasn't drinking.

My brothers, sisters and I went outside to play baseball. We got out our homemade bases and set up a ball diamond in the front yard. That particular day, my dad did something he very rarely did: he played baseball with us.

On Sunday afternoons, he usually slept or drank or just relaxed, but on that Sunday, he came walking outside and grabbed the bat, and we all got excited. Dad was going to play with us. I couldn't believe it.

He got up to bat and hit the ball. Now, my dad was not extremely athletic, so he didn't hit it far, but he was determined to get a homerun every time. So what did he do? He never dropped the bat. He ran around the bases, wielding it like a sword, laughing hysterically, taking a playful swing at anyone who tried to tag him out.

Some of my brothers, determined to get him out during his next at-bat, tried even harder to tag him, but he held them off again with the bat and got yet another homerun. We shouted at him and laughed. We couldn't get enough of this fun side of our father. Soon all of us lay on the ground, laughing until we cried.

When he wasn't drinking, he could have fun. This is a picture of my real dad, the dad that I loved. The dad without alcohol in his blood.

On other days when he was sober, he would pack us younger kids into his convertible. There were eleven of us, but even without the older kids we could barely fit — three or four of us sat around the top edge of the back seat, up on the car. I remember the smell of the summer air, the way the corn rose up on either side of the road and how the dust billowed out behind us.

He drove us to a swimming hole. I splashed around and jumped in off the bank, and everything seemed right with the world. Dad never liked to swim, so he didn't get in with us, but I remember he and Mom sitting there quietly, watching all of us kids play.

I was 12 years old, out riding bicycle with my sister's boyfriend. We drifted down Country Club Road looking for a necklace my sister had lost. It was a beautiful summer day, not too hot with a wonderful breeze, and as we cruised along our eyes focused on the gravel, looking for something shiny.

If you know Country Club Road, you'll know it has a very steep hill. But we only had one bike. So there we were: two guys riding on one bike. Joe-Joe perched on the seat and I was, of all places, on the handlebars. These details were told to me later on. I don't remember a bit of it.

We started cruising down that steep hill, riding double. At the bottom of the hill was a bridge, which we reached at a good clip. That's when the front end of the bike fell apart, and the two of us went flying through the air. Both of us landed on our heads. Black top, as you know, is not very forgiving.

Joe-Joe suffered a fractured skull and was rushed to Lancaster General Hospital. He was unconscious the entire day.

Me? I was knocked out cold, having suffered a serious concussion. I needed 24 stitches to close up my head, lip, and chin. My left eye swelled completely shut. I was covered in road burn on the left side of my body, from the top of my head to the tips of my toes.

I woke up later that day in the hospital, trying to figure out what had happened to me. Doctors and nurses kept asking if I remembered what had happened.

11

"No," I mumbled. I only had one thing on my mind. "Where's my mom?"

I felt so afraid in the hospital, mostly wondering where my mom was. At a time like that, a little boy needs his mother. I knew she could make the hurt go away and take me home. I stayed in the hospital for a week, and my dad eventually brought her to see me a few times in the evenings. I was in such tremendous physical pain, and I couldn't imagine anything feeling worse. Boy, was I wrong!

The day after my accident my dad came in to see me. He brought me a bag of Ruffle's potato chips, my favorite snack. When I saw that he had brought Ruffle's, I thought to myself, "Maybe dad won't be mad at me this time."

But in that hospital room, my dad made a statement that heaped another layer of anger on to the growing pile inside of me. There I was, a little boy, afraid, hurting from head to toe, blind in one eye, wanting in the worst way to go home. Yet my dad, in a very angry tone of voice, turned to me and doled out nothing but blame.

"If you would have listened to me, none of this ever would have happened!"

What I needed at that time from my dad was love and comfort, not a scolding. Yet all I got was further confirmation from him that I wasn't worthy of love or comfort. I was still the no-good person who wouldn't amount to anything.

Chapter Three
A Disappearing Dad

Fi

Many people, looking in on my childhood from the outside, may have thought it was the perfect life, an ideal life. They may have seen this little Amish-Mennonite girl, dressed in her plain dress, hair pulled up under a covering, running barefoot around the farm, and thought, *How could a child in that kind of simple family environment not be perfectly happy?*

Don't get me wrong: many things about my childhood were wonderful. First of all, there were eight of us: Jake, Beck, Anne, Sam, me, Dale, Merrill and Carl. So even though we were poor, there was always someone to play with. I got grouped in with my younger brothers, so I became a tomboy, and I loved playing softball in the summer and ice hockey in the winter.

Living in the country, close to the Chester and Lancaster County line in central Pennsylvania, provided the perfect environment for an animal lover like me. I raised kittens in the barn, and we always had all kinds of dogs on the farm, usually strays that I fed and enticed to hang around. Dad also splurged and bought some ponies, but my younger brothers were scared to ride them, so I pretty much had them all to myself.

I also loved going to market with my mom and dad. In fact, it was at a farmers' market in Philadelphia where I started selling greeting cards and packets of seeds and saved up to buy my first bike. We had a lot of repeat customers, and they just couldn't say *no* when I told them what I was saving up for. I sold hundreds of boxes of greeting cards before I could order my bike, and then I spent weeks waiting in anticipation of its arrival.

When the man finally delivered it, I couldn't open that rattling box full of parts fast enough. I tore at the tape and the cardboard and finally unearthed an instruction manual more complicated than I could imagine. I doubt that Daddy helped me put it together – he just didn't get involved in stuff like that. More than likely my oldest brother Jake gave me a hand. It was a beautiful, black 3-speed, and I kept that thing shined and clean. My bike opened up a whole new world for me.

Freedom. I loved riding the five miles to school. If I close my eyes and think about it now, I can still smell the air and feel the wind against my face. I didn't have many morning chores, but I do remember washing the breakfast dishes as fast as possible so that I could get outside and on to my bike. Some days I would just head out, ride all over the countryside – everything felt so wide open, nothing like the confined space of our farmhouse where I shared a bed with my two sisters. I don't think I even told anyone where I went.

That's probably when I started to realize that making money also afforded some of its own freedom. I made $5 every time I washed Jake's car – I was the only one he let wash it, and I took pride in that. $3 of that $5 went to mom and dad, and of course I didn't get paid to work for them at market. That's just how things were back then. Every family was forced to operate as a unit and work together if there was going to be food on the table.

But the money I was allowed to keep from cleaning Jake's car went towards another big purchase: my first radio. As a young Amish-Mennonite girl, I wasn't allowed to have a radio. Worldly music was a big no-no. So actually, what I bought was an alarm clock (it just happened to have a radio feature).

Yet, darkness clung to my childhood. That I cannot deny. As I got older, I'd find myself in bed in the middle of the day, bawling my eyes out with no idea where the sadness came from. Or I'd be working in the barns, and something as little as a stubbed toe would make me so angry that I wouldn't have hesitated to hurt someone. Some of the contributors to my emotional instability were obvious, things that can be easily identified. But other parts of my deep-seeded unhappiness were unclear and hidden under the surface.

Take my dad's recurring depression, for example. There were instances where he disappeared for an hour, or an afternoon, or an entire day. He would simply walk off when no one was looking, and we had no idea where he went.

"Daddy's not here," Mom would say, or "Eli's gone." Whatever she said, there was always fear in her voice, and we knew what it meant. Each time he disappeared, a little bit of darkness descended into my mind. Where was he? Why was he gone? Would we find him dead?

That last question summed up my greatest fear and kept me in the house while everyone else went out

15

looking for him. I was afraid to look. I didn't want to find him dead: an Amish viewing (before the funeral took place) was held in the person's house, and the thought of having his body lying in our house became my worst nightmare. His frequent disappearances made me feel insecure and vulnerable.

When he walked back into the house, everyone acted like nothing had happened. I can't even remember exactly how I felt, other than relieved. I don't remember feeling angry with him for disappearing. But every time I arrived somewhere expecting to see him, yet not finding him, I felt a fear rise up in me: was he gone again? Would he come back? Would we find him dead?

Now, I realize that he was depressed. There were so many mouths to feed and rarely enough money. He tried business venture after business venture and almost always failed. If he bought a herd of pigs, they would catch a rare disease, and most of them would die. If he bought a flourishing market stand, something uncommon would happen and cause the business in that market to go elsewhere. Or he'd sell the stand prematurely, make a little bit of money but miss out on the jackpot. He was a millionaire at heart, but for most of his life, it never panned out for him.

I loved my daddy. He was a fun guy and definitely the parent that played with us the most. He got dentures at an early age, and he'd take them out and chase us around, gnawing on our toes with his bare gums until it hurt. He scared us and invigorated us, all at the same time. That was his idea of playtime, and it was fun.

Sometimes he'd take us to a swimming hole at a nearby pond – it had a diving board and a small pier. He'd pack all the kids into the car and drive us there, maybe two miles away, and at the end of a long day working outside, that cold water felt like heaven. Jumping off the pier into the water, disappearing into the stillness and the quiet and the cold of the pond...sometimes I just wanted to stay under. Stay hidden.

Daddy would sit there on the dock and smile or chase us around and try to throw us in. Having him around was like being in the presence of a jolly storm – you never knew if he was going to sweep you up and carry you away or throw you into the water.

He didn't hide his feelings very well – his eyes gave him away. So did his hat. You could tell his mood by the way he wore it: straight up and tall meant he was feeling good; if it was cocked to the side he was either tired, discouraged or depressed.

But in spite of his lack of success, he had very few enemies and a lot of friends, remarkable when you take into consideration how he pushed the limits: at church, at my school, in business – he told people what he thought, and he did what he wanted to do.

My mom was a wonderful cook who knew how to make delicious food on an extremely limited budget. Dad, the social one of the two, would often invite people home from church without telling her, and she stretched the food so that everyone had plenty.

Our family used to sit around our huge table every night for dinner. Sometimes, Mom bought ice cream and sliced it down so that each of us could have one melting piece. Together, my parents gave me a strong foundation on which to build my life.

In the winter, mom hosted taffy-pulling parties for our youth group at church. She made the taffy on the stove, and when it cooled we paired up and stretched it over and over again. There were 30 or 40 of us, talking and shouting, the entire table covered with taffy.

One Christmas Eve, my parents came home from market, and Dad got out our gift (most years, all eight of us received one gift to share): a racecar track. He set it up, and it nearly filled an entire room of our house. The small cars zipped around, like tiny, live things trying to escape. What a great present! We stayed awake all night racing cars, and Dad was right there beside us, his laugh sounding out through the house like a church bell.

Still, his occasional disappearances weighed heavily on my mind. In the midst of a peaceful life the seeds of depression, anxiety and anger found soil.

Chapter Four
Promises to an Unknown God

Mike

There was something my dad always used to tell me, and the way he said it seared the words into my mind:

"You'll never amount to anything," he said spitefully, as if trying to quench any ember of hope that might have somehow grown inside of me at an early age. (Of course, the words he used were not as clean as the version I've given you.) That's just the way he was. That's the way he operated when he was drunk.

Maybe he said it because he was disappointed with his own life. Maybe he actually believed it. I don't know. He said it to all of us, condemning his own children to meaningless lives, attempting to convince us over and over again how pointless it was to even try.

Dad was a very angry person. When you have to quit school in 4th grade to go work and help out the family (like he did), and you have low self-esteem, you're not going to like people. Not your wife, not your kids. Not anybody. His own dad treated him the same way that he treated us. When you grow up in an alcoholic family like he did, like I did, you have two options: you either live the same exact life yourself, or you fight it.

He lived the same life. I fought it.

Whatever the reason, whatever his intended result, my father's words did one thing: they motivated me. I decided to fight against living that life of drunkenness and negativity. Every time he said that, I burned with anger and a stubborn belief that I would not be worthless. I clenched my jaw, and deep inside of me, I silently screamed back at him.

"I am going to prove you wrong!"

And I did.

That statement gave me the fuel I needed to move forward in my life and make something of myself. We lived in a home that wasn't nice. Kids at school used to call us white trash. And I hated it. I used to think to myself: *Someday I'm going to have something much, much better than this.*

Mornings started quietly. Dad woke me up at 5:30am to start the fires to warm the house. Why me? I don't know. I remember him putting me in charge of the house one time when he went away. There was no way my older brothers would listen to me – why should they? Dad wasn't too happy about that, so when he got home and found out that they hadn't completed their normal duties, he took off his belt and beat me. As if I could control my older brothers! Later he stood and watched as mom covered the red lines and bruises on my back with salve, not saying a word.

Why me?

But with my dad, it was always the alcohol. When he managed to stay sober for short stretches of time, he became a different person: kind, loving, and respectful towards my mom. It was like Jekyl and Hyde. As soon as he got some alcohol in him, he became one of the meanest, most violent and confrontational men I knew.

Every morning, I made the coffee and took it up to Mom and Dad. Then Mom made us breakfast, and we shoveled it in before walking a mile to the bus stop. When I was thirteen, I started working on a neighboring farm to make some money, so I got up at 4:30am, rode my bike five miles to work at that farm, then came home and got ready for school. I don't think I ever felt angry about working – in fact, the small amount of money I made gave me a sense of independence.

One day, when I was around twelve years old, I got home from school and the house was all torn up. Dad had decided not to go to work that day – instead, he went out and got drunk on wine, which made him meaner than anything else. Then, he took the hatchet and cut up some of our furniture before taking all the food out of the cupboards, throwing it on the floor, and destroying it. Then, he threw the dishes into a big pile and broke every one.

My five-year-old brother was in the big freestanding bathtub we had perched in the middle of the kitchen, watching the whole thing happen. We saw things that no kid should have to witness, and that kind of thing changes a child.

By the time I got home that day, Dad was out in the orchard sleeping under an apple tree. The sun shone and a breeze rustled the leaves. We walked around like mice when the cat's asleep. I don't know how long he lay there, but we didn't want to wake him. I didn't care if he slept all day.

"Mike!" My mom shouted from inside the house. "Where did you put the knives?"

I wedged the axe into the next piece of wood I was going to split and walked inside. Once, when my dad was drunk, he had gotten into a fight with one of my older brothers. Eventually Dad had pinned him down on the floor and started choking him, then jumped to his feet and ran to the kitchen, shouting, "I'm going to get the butcher knife and finish you off!" Ever since that day, I started hiding the knives.

I'm not telling this story to make my dad look like a terrible monster, but I do want you to understand what alcohol does to a person's demeanor and personality. When my dad was sober, he would give you the shirt off his back. That's just the kind of person he was when he wasn't drinking.

I remember one time my dad and I were outside, and he found a cardinal frozen nearly solid. He actually brought that beautiful bird inside and thawed it out, kept it alive, and nursed it back to health. Eventually, we found a birdcage, and I remember waking up in the morning to the sound of that cardinal singing in the living room.

Another time in the winter, we passed two older people walking down the highway. He picked them up and brought them home, and my mom made them a hot meal. Then my dad drove them to wherever it was they were headed.

The problem with me hiding the knives came when Mom wanted to cook and she couldn't find them. I went up the stairs and into one of the bedrooms and pulled three or four knives out from under the mattress, then carried them downstairs and handed them to Mom.

She smiled and shook her head. I was around eight years old at the time.

That night I walked into the kitchen. Mom held the telephone up against her ear. At first I couldn't tell who she was talking to, but then this look of horror spread over her face. I still remember that look.

She hung up the phone and looked at me.

"Dad said he's coming home, and he's going to kill all seven of his sons."

That was enough to get all of us out the door. My younger brothers and I ran out to a log cabin that we had built in the woods. In those days, we spent a lot of time out there playing, sometimes from morning to night. It wasn't unusual for us to camp out and sleep in the cabin we built.

We stayed out there for two nights after that phone call. We sat in our log cabin, quietly listening. Every cracking branch I heard, every stirring of the leaves, I was sure my father had arrived. Eventually we crept back close to the house and waited to see if he was still on one of his rampages. I'm not sure what ended up tipping us off that the coast was clear, but at some point we walked back into the house.

As usual, Mom and Dad acted like nothing had happened.

Through all of this, one desire began to build stronger and stronger inside of me, this resolve that I just couldn't shake: as soon as I could, I would leave. I had grown so tired of the violence, the alcohol, and the atmosphere of hopelessness. I returned home one afternoon to find my dad and two of my brothers fighting in the bathroom, once again nearly killing each other.

They were on the floor, their legs and bodies and arms tangled up and flailing. Punches were thrown. More shouts. I remember, as clear as day, pleading with a God I didn't even know existed:

God, if you will ever get me out of this mess, I will spend the rest of my life helping people out of their messes.

How can I explain this? I didn't go to church. I didn't know anything about God. I certainly didn't believe in God. I didn't want to be a counselor, and never before had I considered helping other people "out of their messes." Yet there I was, a young boy, crying out for help. Making promises to God.

Somehow, on that day, God heard the voice of a boy on a farm in central Pennsylvania. Nothing changed overnight, but now, as I look back on the course my life took, I realize that someone began setting things in motion that would deliver me from that environment, giving me a hope and a future.

Three or four years later, when I was sixteen, the man who owned the farm where I worked moved on and no longer needed me. I was disappointed – I enjoyed working on farms, and it was good money. At the time, it seemed like a lousy bit of news, but looking back I can now see how that one decision was God intervening in my life and helping to "get me out of this mess."

"You should go talk to Donnie," my previous employer said. "He might want a hired man."

I shook his hand and walked back to my car: a '57 Cadillac that smoked so bad out the back that if you were driving behind me, you were in trouble. It was a big old rattletrap of a car, and I loved it.

Anyway, I rumbled up Donnie's lane and knocked on the door, full of confidence. He answered.

"Hi there," I said. "Are you Donnie?"

He nodded, shaking my hand.

"What can I do for you?" he asked.

"I'm looking for work. My old boss, he's moving on, and he said you might be looking for a hired man."

Donnie stared down at the ground for a moment, then looked up at me.

"Sorry, son, not right now. I think I've got the work covered on my own."

"Are you sure, man? I'm a hard worker and can do pretty much everything. I've been working at that farm for three years."

"Nah, sorry kid. We're not looking for a hired man."

But he wasn't convincing, and I continued asking him. I probably drove down Donnie's lane once a week – I wanted a job, and I loved farming. There was something about plowing or planting a field that fed my soul. Finally, during my fourth or fifth try, Donnie gave in.

"Hey, mister," I said, standing on his doorstep yet again. "Just coming by to see if you're ready to take on a hired man yet."

He squinted and scratched the back of his head.

"You sure are persistent, kid," he said.

"Yes, sir."

He paused for a moment.

"Okay," he said. "Come by on Monday, early."

I started working for Donnie before and after school. I helped milk the cows, and in the spring, I drove the plow. I worked out in those fields until dark. Saturday was the same thing, except it was all day. I worked Sundays, too: Donnie didn't want me doing the normal work on the Sabbath, but the cows still had to be milked.

Donnie and his wife Dorcas had three children: a little boy around five, a little girl about four, and then a baby named Suzie. She was just an infant when I started working there – she became my little sister, since I ended up working there for about ten years. I watched those kids grow up, and the family took me in.

But at home it was business as usual. By this time I was sixteen years old and many of my brothers and sisters were married and out of the house – getting married was one of the ways of escaping that environment. Each of us took baggage along to our new lives, whether it was alcoholism or anger, dependency or depression. But one thing hadn't changed: my dad still went to the Speakman and got drunk. He still came home and tore things apart. Every once in a while Mom would have a black eye, and I didn't have to ask her to find out where she got it.

Something changed in me, though. As I got older, I started to voice my displeasure to my dad about his drinking, something that resulted in argument after argument. I'd put a word in here, a word in there, criticizing him for getting drunk and getting into fights. He hated that, and we always ended up yelling at each other.

We argued about school a lot, too. He wanted me to stay home, to work more, and I wanted to go to school, mostly because working harder for Dad just meant he would have more money to drink. Those pointless discussions just went round and round – if you want to experience frustration, argue with a drunk.

Yet for some reason we never fought physically – I was one of my dad's sons that he seemed disinterested in punching. You'd think that with his volatile behavior, his willingness to fight with my brothers, and my own growing confidence and more vocal displeasure, we would end up having some kind of physical altercation. But that never happened.

Back at the farm, Donnie paid me $50 a week, which in 1967 was pretty good money. I gave most of it to my parents – one week I gave it all to them except for a few dollars. It was pretty normal in those days for kids to give the money they made to their parents, but the thing I didn't like was that, as I expected, Dad vanished, off to the Speakman with my money. He got drunk with it. I tried to get ahead in life, but he just drank.

At that point, I convinced them to let me quit school.

"I'll work full-time," I told my dad, who needed no convincing. He probably imagined all the extra money coming in, how much easier it would make his own life. But he didn't know my plan.

About a month after I left school, I chatted with Donnie.

"I've talked it over with my wife," Donnie said. "Why don't you come live with us? We have an extra room. You can stay there. We'll give you a bedroom and food, and you can keep working here."

Huh, I thought. *Maybe I could do that.*

Donnie knew my family situation. He knew the deal with my dad and my brothers. I think he wanted to offer me a way out of it. In the back of my mind, I remembered the promise I had made to God: *If you get me out of this mess...* So I took him up on his offer and decided to move in to Donnie's place.

Of course my dad totally bucked against that idea. He didn't like it one bit. I'd like to think he didn't want me to move out because he would miss me, but I know the money I brought home influenced his reaction, too.

"This is your home!" he argued. "You don't have to live there."

Even after I had moved out and lived with Donnie's family for quite some time, Dad still got upset when I said, "Well, I guess I better head home."

"Isn't this your home?" he'd ask, getting angry.

"Not anymore," I said, shrugging.

When I first moved in with Donnie, relief settled on me immediately. To be in a family where they didn't drink and argue, where they went to church together every Sunday and left me sitting in a completely silent house? The whole place exuded peace. Everything felt calm. I didn't have to worry about whether or not we'd have food to eat because they always provided. It wasn't as if I had ever gone hungry at my parent's house, but for some reason I always had that worry. The serenity of Donnie's farm, in contrast with the house where I grew up, amazed me.

But I remained the same person. There were times when Donnie and I just didn't see eye to eye, and I hated that feeling because it made me feel like I was back home again. I'm telling you – the arguments I had with Donnie about work put me in a funk, and I would sometimes go two weeks without talking. We often stood side by side in the fields and in the barn, but I'd work without saying a word.

A lot of times this came about because I stayed out so late at night. I think he wanted me to work all day, eat dinner at night, and then go to bed and get some rest, but I was a teenager. I wasn't going to do that. I worked all day, ate dinner, and then stayed out late into the night, often getting no more than three or four hours of sleep before waking up to start it all over again. Night after night.

Maybe Donnie thought it affected my work. Maybe he knew the crowd I ran around with and thought I was better off staying at home. I didn't think my nightlife affected my work, but maybe he was right. I don't know. He got on my case about it, and then we argued, something that was difficult for me to handle emotionally, given my background and the stuff I grew up with. I found myself feeling pretty low – I don't know if it was depression or exhaustion, but so much of the time I felt like I was living in a haze without a lot of hope. I was very sad inside and didn't have a lot to live for.

It certainly wasn't all Donnie; it wasn't even mostly Donnie. I wasn't the nicest guy, still pretty rough around the edges. I didn't go to church with them on Sundays even though they invited me every week and talked to me about Jesus every chance they got. Donnie's wife spoke gently, witnessing with a quiet spirit. But Donnie was all fire and brimstone, a real Bible-thumper. I used to cuss at him when he tried to talk to me about how I was living.

Then in August of 1968, something changed. Seventeen years old, I had lived with them for about a year at that point.

"You really should come with us to church," Donnie said. "Jesus loves you, Mike."

I said a few choice words and ended it the way I usually did.

"You can have your Jesus, and I'll have my fun. Don't bother me with that stuff, Donnie."

We were milking cows, and he stopped, looked me in the eyes.

"If you die today, if you go out with those so-called friends of yours on the highway and crash your car and die, did you know that unless you know Jesus you are going to hell?"

I looked at Donnie. That statement tore through me.

Unless you know Jesus, you are going to hell.

"I never knew that," I said, turning away slowly and walking back into the barn.

Chapter Five
Turning Off My Emotions

Fi

So much of who I became was a reaction against the way I was raised. Sometimes I saw my mom cry because we didn't have enough money, so I worked hard at a young age to make money. I worked at Bill's diner when I was 12 years old, washing dishes with my older sister Anne. Bill also drove school buses, and when he saw how I cleaned, he paid me to wash out the inside of his school buses. I scrubbed all those seats by hand and loved how the windows glistened. That's probably where I learned how to clean glass without leaving streaks.

If my dad mowed the grass, he didn't trim the edges, and he mowed every which way, something that drove me crazy. Today I want everything to be just so. Mom didn't focus a lot on cleaning – how could she, with eight of us running around – so I did a lot of the housework. I always told myself, "When I get older, my house will not be this messy." I responded to their lack of organization by becoming a perfectionist.

My dad also started more projects than you can imagine without ever finishing one of them! He bought these second-hand lawn mowers but never got them serviced – if you wanted to mow, it was never as simple as going outside and starting the mower because at least one small thing was always wrong with every single one of them. Then, because we didn't have a working mower, the grass got out of hand. There was the time he installed two light posts at each corner of a concrete patio that he built – they looked really nice. But they never worked! He just never finished the wiring.

I only mention these things because I'm trying to explain the internal frustration (that often turned into anger) burning in me – sometimes it was an insignificant response to my dad not finishing a project or because of a messy house. But at other times it was this deep, burning anger against an enemy I couldn't pinpoint – I just wanted to punch the air and scream at the sky. Something inside me was almost always angry: it would flare up, and then it would lie dormant, but it was there. I couldn't explain or understand it.

It wasn't until that phone call during the winter of 1997 that the final puzzle piece came into the picture. In the mean time, I struggled with my feelings, battled my anger. I turned off my emotions for long periods of time by simply disengaging from what went on around me. I structured my mind so that events that brought other people to tears didn't affect me. I discovered something about myself: emotions annoyed me, and I could shut them down. Everything except anger – the anger I couldn't eliminate.

I don't think a person can survive like this for very long. Closing out emotions leads to a coldness and eventually despair. Bottled up anger comes out in some form or another. But in those days, stopping my emotions seemed the least painful option.

My parents, in spite of being poor themselves, took many trips to a soup kitchen in New York City to help the homeless. We kids would usually go along, and often my two sisters and I would sing for the men in the shelter. During this time, I began to enjoy the feeling of performing. I saw how happy my singing made people. It filled me with a purpose that I rarely felt otherwise.

Sometimes, too, my parents brought these men into our home, one at a time. They'd put them up in the barn or the attic and try to help them get a fresh start. The men worked on our farm or somewhere in town. They never stayed long, and some of them we rarely saw. I was thirteen years old, and those strange men scared me. Their presence made me nervous.

One of the men my parents brought home from the soup kitchen befriended me. He took an interest in me that felt like kindness. I can still see his face. He asked about my bike and my ponies and showed me some things around the farm. He seemed like a nice guy. Then one day, he showed me pornographic pictures.

The images are still burned in my mind – it's amazing how long those things stay with you. I tried to avoid him, and he wasn't around much longer. But I never told anyone. It was one more secret, one more wound, one more reason for the anger inside of me to grow. It also reinforced something in my mind: I started associating men with guilty condemnation and sex with lewd, dirty acts. I didn't know it at the time, but these things were creating a difficult foundation on which to build a marriage.

I was 15 when my two older sisters got married. The three of us had slept in the same bed for as long as I could remember, and the first night I went to bed alone was a sad night for me. I missed them so much that I wept, my tears forming a wet spot on my pillow.

My sister Becky and her husband Aaron moved to a farm, and on many afternoons I went over to help them. I loved being outside and driving the tractor, plowing fields. I milked the cows for them. The spring hummed with activity as we prepared the fields and started planting crops. In the summer, I helped them bale hay. The hot sun beat down on us, and sweat drenched me in minutes, but I enjoyed being outside, even in the heat. An immense feeling of gratification came with hard work.

My brother-in-law Aaron was very organized and kept a tidy farm, the kind of place I enjoyed working. Becky seemed to enjoy my help around the house. In some ways their house was the kind of home I wished for, and I loved spending time with them.

In the winter, my younger brothers and I went ice-skating every single night, as long as a thick enough layer of ice coated the pond. We'd race out the door with our skates, and I'd play hockey with the boys. At the end of the night, we'd "crack the whip" – all of us would link hands and skate in a circle. The person at the end of the "whip" would get shot out like a cannonball across the ice.

The winters stretched longer and colder then, at least in my memory, and thinking back on those dark, freezing nights, remembering the way my lungs burned and my breath escaped in cloudy bursts, it still fills me with a sense of excitement and happiness.

When I was 17, I left the Amish-Mennonite church. It wasn't a huge deal for my parents because my dad struggled for years to abide by all the rules, and a few of my brothers and sisters had already left the Amish by that time anyway. So my choice to leave caused little disruption.

33

But I do remember my dad's thoughts on girls having short hair.

"I don't ever want to see you come into my house with bangs or short hair!" he'd say, practically fuming at the thought that any of his girls would become that worldly.

Those were the exact words he used. For years I was scared to cut my hair short, and when I finally did, the last person I wanted to see was my dad. The funny thing is, I can't remember his reaction — it must not have been as bad as he had promised.

When I left the Amish-Mennonite church, I started going to a local charismatic church with my brothers and sisters. My two sisters and I began traveling around the area, singing at other churches. The interesting thing is that my dad pushed us into singing. He loved music. When the three of us had been young and supposed to be sleeping, we sang together in our shared bed at night, and every time my parents had company to the house, my dad had always asked us to sing for our guests.

The pastor at our new church was dynamic and assertive. His personality drew people from all over the county, and soon our church was bursting at the seams with young converts, ready to change the world. We started going to church almost every night of the week. A palpable excitement spread throughout the area — people's lives were being changed for the better at that church, and I enjoyed seeing that happen.

Soon after that, a young man's name started coming up on my radar, mostly mentioned by some of my girlfriends: Mike Lusby. Before long, we met.

Chapter Six
Meeting God, and Meeting Fi

Mike

"If you die today, if you go out on the highway and crash your car and die, did you know that unless you know Jesus you are going to hell?"

That question came to me again and again, all day and through the night. I can't say I thought about it constantly, but as soon as my thoughts went into idle, that sentence rushed in. I was going to hell. Perhaps the strangest thing of all was that it made sense to me. I had stepped foot in church only a few times – I remember once, when I was about ten years old, going to a Bible camp at a local Mennonite church. Maybe that's why when I was ten I cried out to God.

The question Donnie posed made sense in my mind: how could someone who lived like I did, partied and fought like I did, and treated other people as poorly as I did, expect to get into heaven?

My life revolved around the guys I hung out with at school and the fights we got into. We tore up and down the countryside looking for trouble – that was my life. I worked hard, and I played hard. My friends and I judged each other by how often we swore and how tough we fought. Other people saw us coming down the street in Coatesville, and they turned around, avoided us. And that's how we liked it.

That night at Donnie's, sleep didn't come to me right away. I tossed and turned and stared through the dark at a ceiling I could barely see. I thought back over my life, how I had ended up where I was. I remembered the time I had called out to God, made that promise.

God, if you get me out of this mess, I will spend the rest of my life getting people out of their messes.

For the first time, I wondered where my life was going. Was there a God? Had he heard me that day? I certainly felt like something, or someone, had delivered me from the mess that my life used to be. What was my purpose? Finally, I drifted off to sleep.

I dreamed that my friends and I hiked up a tall mountain, and eventually we made it to the top. As usual, a bunch of guys from another school entered the scene, and we fought. In most fights, I held my own pretty well. But in that fight, in my dream, I got hit and knocked off of a cliff.

I felt that falling sensation, my arms and legs flailing, the mountaintop moving away from me. I knew that behind me, somewhere beneath me, the ground rushed up. My body would smash on to the rocks. I screamed, as loud as I could.

"Don't let me die! God, don't let me die! I don't want to go to hell!"

I sat straight up in bed, still screaming when I woke up. I looked around. Darkness. I hadn't died. I felt the sweat on my forehead. My breathing came fast and heavy with relief. I wasn't going to hell…yet.

I knew it was time to milk the cows, so I climbed out of bed, got dressed and walked through the dark, out to the barn. My hands shook, and I shoved them deep into my pockets. It was a warm August morning, and I could tell it was going to get hot. Donnie met me in the barn, and we proceeded to go through our morning routine. We rarely talked on those early mornings, probably because I was usually pretty tired and often because Donnie was upset at me for staying out so late the night before.

Then, the morning light began creeping in through the large windows, illuminating the specs of dust that floated through the sunbeams. I liked mornings – it was hard getting out of bed, but there was something rewarding about an early start, working hard, and making my way in the world.

As we finished up, I turned to him.

"You know, is there any possibility that I can go see your preacher tonight?"

I didn't even know why. It just seemed the right thing to do.

"Sure," Donnie said in an even voice. "I can make arrangements for that."

I sighed, surprised at the amount of relief that I felt.

That afternoon, I called my brother Joe, one of my closest friends at the time. We got into everything together. Three years younger than me, Joe experienced everything I had at home.

"Hey, Joe," I told him. "I'm going to see the preacher tonight. You want to go with me?"

"Sure, why not?"

Joe and I were tight. If I would have said, "Hey, you want to go jump off that cliff with me?" he would have said, "Sure, why not?" Anyway, that's how I remember him, willing to follow me anywhere, but he might not agree with that.

So Joe and I went to see Melville Nafsinger, one of the pastors at Maple Grove Mennonite Church. Melville must have wondered what was going on — here were two of the toughest roughnecks in the area, coming into his house, wanting to hear about God. What he didn't realize was that we were about to become the two easiest converts he ever spoke to. He sat us down in the living room and looked at me first.

"Donnie said you wanted to meet with me, Michael. What can I do for you?"

I cut straight to the chase.

"Man," I said, "I don't know what I got to do, but I don't want to go to hell."

Nothing about my announcement surprised him, which was a great relief to me. I had been wondering about his reaction — I had never spoken to a real, live preacher before. Would he laugh at the idea that I could avoid hell? Would he shake his head and say I wasn't good enough? But he did neither of these things.

He explained a little bit of the Gospel to me, the basic stuff. Before I knew it, he had Joe and I on our knees beside some chairs right there in his living room, praying the sinner's prayer. I had no clue what I was saying at the time, but in that moment he led us to Jesus. Eventually, Joe and I left Melville's house and headed home.

Something in me felt different. Lighter somehow, as if I had been carrying something for a long, long time, and then someone came up to me and offered to carry it for me. I couldn't explain it in words, and if someone would have asked me what I had just done, I wouldn't have been able to tell them. But it felt good.

As I walked into the house, Donnie asked me something.

"Well, how about you come with us to church on Sunday?"

"Okay," I agreed, because that seemed the right thing to say, but inside I wasn't too crazy about the idea. All throughout the week thoughts swirled through my mind: *Why would I go to church? Why do I even want to go? What will my friends say?* All this stuff went through my head.

But on Sunday morning, I went anyway.

I remember this precious lady – her name was Francis Stoltzfus. What a lady! What a saint of God. She was a little bitty woman, Mennonite, dressed plain and wearing a covering, very soft-spoken and kind. She prayed for Joe and I often throughout the years, and when she saw me in church on my first day, she came right up and said something that changed my life. I still think of her words often, and they have a huge affect on me:

"Now that you've become a Christian, I bet the devil's just harassing your mind, isn't he? Probably telling you that you shouldn't go to church? Asking you what your friends are going to think?"

Her feisty little voice had fire in it and a wisdom that gripped me. There was something immensely joyful about her questions, as if she would have gladly entered the battlefield of the mind for the sake of Jesus. Amazement poured through me. This tiny woman knew the very thoughts going through my mind!

"Is that where those thoughts are coming from?" I asked her, completely taken aback. "Is that who's putting those thoughts in my head?"

"He's here to steal, kill and destroy. And he'll start in your mind."

It made me so mad at Satan. In fact, the words and thoughts he tried to plant in my brain brought about the same affect that my dad's words did about me being a failure:

You'll never amount to nothing! My dad's voice screamed in my head.

I'll prove you wrong, dad.

Don't go to church! What are your friends going to say? The Devil tried to trick me out of a good life.

I'm going to church. I don't care what anyone says.

I decided to live a good life for God, no matter how much junk Satan put in my head. It was the fighter in me, strong and stubborn and determined.

Francis Stoltzfus died in a car crash not long ago. When I heard about her passing, I felt the sadness that you feel when someone who impacted your life is no longer around. But the things she said and the ways she encouraged me carry on into eternity.

Joe and I both got involved in the youth group at Maple Grove Mennonite Church right away. We both bought Martin guitars and loved to sing, so that was kind of what we became known for. We started traveling around to all the Mennonite socials and youth groups to sing. There was a fairly popular trio in the area that asked us to come in and open for their concerts sometimes.

We sang some gospel songs – there were about 25 that we actually wrote together, songs that we made up in our heads and never wrote down. We sang some Everly Brothers and some of Elvis's stuff. Things like that. Sometimes I'd tell a few jokes, and then we'd sing. Soon we performed three to four evenings a week.

After these mini-concerts, we'd go to The Green Lantern, a little dive that sold delicious cheese steak sandwiches. Joe and I went in there and got a huge sandwich with an order of fries, shoved it down, then looked at each other with big old grins on our faces.

"I think I can do another one!" one of us would say, and we'd laugh until our sides ached and order another meal. We had fun together in those days – I think it was because of our brand new life in Christ. We felt free.

Not that our new life in the church was completely without its troubles.

You have to remember that in those days the family we had been raised in was referred to as heathen. We didn't have a churched upbringing. People in that small town knew where everyone came from, and I guess we were pretty easy to spot, especially when we ended up going to a Mennonite church.

Being teenagers, we were ready to date girls, but there was some disappointment when we realized that the parents of these Mennonite girls weren't too happy with the idea of their girls going out with us. They were happy to welcome us into their church and pleased at the idea that we became Christians, but the prevailing attitude seemed to be, *Don't even think about dating our girls.*

I look back now, and it's easy for me to have grace. They probably looked at Joe and I, along with the fact that we came from an alcoholic, abusive family, and thought we wouldn't make it. That's the kind of family that we came from, so what would keep us from going back, falling, messing up? What they didn't know was that we didn't have anything to go back to – our only option was forward.

There was one girl – I'll call her Laura. She and I started dating, and we hung out all the time. We actually got pretty serious. Her father was a farmer. Sometimes she'd come over to Donnie's farm on Sunday nights and help me milk the cows. We really liked each other.

Her dad let that happen for a while, until it was time for her to leave for college. Then one night, she said she needed to talk to me.

"We have to break up, Mike," she said with tears in her eyes.

"What?" Complete shock numbed my body.

"My dad said that if we don't break up, he won't pay for my college education."

It was so painful for me – she was the first Christian girl that I ever really, really liked. But we broke up, and I moved on. I didn't realize it back then, but I know it today: some things are just not meant to be. I have no hard feelings toward Laura's family. God has a perfect will for us, and He allows things to happen to keep us on track.

When God transforms you, watch out – it's amazing! The eternal security of my parents and siblings became my number one concern. *What would happen to them if they died?* So after Joe and I got saved and started going to church, we witnessed to the rest of our family. In some ways my arguments with my dad grew even more heated – now they involved religion, Christianity, and the path of a moral life. He certainly didn't want to talk about that, especially if I caught him after drinking too much.

Then one week, our church held a revival meeting, and people packed into that place every night to hear this dynamic Mennonite preacher. Fire practically shot out from him as he spoke – he was a real evangelist. Somehow, I convinced my mom and dad to attend.

His preaching split the air that night, and I prayed and prayed for my parents throughout the entire service, that they would find God. It was summer time and hot as anything. People packed that place so full that they ended up standing around the back, but in the silences left by the preacher's pauses, you could hear the wind blowing through the trees and the insects chirping. Everyone sat or stood completely still.

At the end of the night, the preacher gave an altar call, asking if anyone wanted to follow Christ. Mom and Dad stood up, but the aisle was so full of people making a decision to follow Christ that they couldn't get to the front. They were stuck halfway, close to where I sat, so I stood up and walked over to them.

That night, in Maple Grove Mennonite Church, I prayed the same prayer with my parents that Melville had prayed with me. My dad changed a lot, and life for him and my mom became so much better. He stopped drinking and smoking, and my mom said that the last twenty years of their marriage was the happiest time of her life. That night was one of the best nights of my life.

Not too long after I made the decision to follow Christ, I sat in Maple Grove on a Sunday night. The church had organized a special singing program, led by a local family. They were what we called Beachy Amish, or Amish-Mennonite, and they dressed in plain clothing. The women and girls wore coverings very similar to the Amish.

I sat there listening to their voices rise through the church. The whole family was lined up on stage, singing their hearts out. I loved music, and this kind of stuff always got my attention. You also have to keep in mind that I was so new to the church that I sat up at the front for every service.

One of the girls on the opposite side of the stage sang a solo, and she immediately caught my attention. She was about fifteen years old, and that girl could belt it out. I remember in particular one of the high parts in one of the songs, and she nailed it.

There is something about that girl that I really like, I thought to myself. *Wow.*

I always loved music and especially loved the idea of marrying a girl who could sing, but I didn't look at her in that way, at least not during that first time I saw her. She was just a young girl, and I didn't understand the way she dressed or what her family was about. But in spite of all that, her voice bowled me over.

I picked up the church bulletin to see what her name was.

Fi Smucker.

But I was only 17 at the time, so she was probably only 15. It's strange to think that seven years later the two of us would be saying our wedding vows. For a long time, I just could not get her singing out of my mind. But it would be the last time I saw her for many years.

43

Then, in 1970, I went to the Mennonite Voluntary Service in Anderson, South Carolina. My roommate knew a girl from Lancaster County, the next county over from where I had grown up: someone I'll call Molly. She came down to visit my roommate a few times, and we started writing back and forth and went out on a few dates. In the letters we exchanged, she often wrote about her best friend: Fi Smucker.

They were such good friends, and Molly went on and on about this girl and how much time they spent together. I found it hard to believe that this might be the same girl I heard sing a few years before, but I couldn't imagine that there were very many Fi Smuckers in the world.

During one of my visits home, Molly asked if I wanted to go with her to church.

"Okay," I said. "Sure. That sounds like fun."

"Great!" she said. "I can't wait to introduce you to my best friend, Fi."

When I got to church, I looked all over for Fi but didn't see her. I still had this mental picture of the fifteen-year-old girl singing on stage, dressed in her Amish-Mennonite garb. Then Molly came walking up to me, accompanied by a gorgeous girl with dark hair and dark eyes and a beautiful smile.

"Hi, Mike!" Molly said. "This is my friend, Fi."

My eyes probably popped out of my head because the Fi I remembered had been dressed in plain clothes and wore a covering, but this girl wasn't plain at all. What I didn't realize was that in the months leading up to that point, Fi had left the Amish-Mennonite church.

Whew, I thought. *This girl sure is pretty.*

Fi attended Victory Chapel, but at the time, I still went to Maple Grove Mennonite. She came across as a very spiritual person; after all, she traveled around to sing about Jesus and had grown up in the conservative community. Meanwhile, I was recently saved out of a pretty rough life. I convinced myself that there was no way I could ever date her – she was way too spiritual, so far above me.

When I got back from the Mennonite Voluntary Service in 1972, I continued working with Donnie on the farm and started hanging out with his sister – I was 19 and she was 16. Donnie's dad never told me specifically that he didn't think it appropriate for me to date his daughter, but he was always suggesting others girls for me to date. One day his suggestion surprised me.

"Hey, Mike, do you know that Fi Smucker girl over there at Victory Chapel? She's not dating anyone. Why don't you go on a date with her?"

Absolutely not, I told myself. *I'm not making a fool of myself. She'd never go out with me!*

But he kept asking me, just about every week. He probably noticed my reaction when he first asked me about her.

"Did you ask Fi out yet?"

I laughed.

"No way! Why would she want to go out with me? She's way more spiritual than me."

But then one day I started thinking about it: why not? Why not ask her out? What difference did it make if she said "no"?

I think I called her on the phone in the spring of '73, because I was kind of a chicken. I thought she would say no. I was sure she would be polite about it, but "no" was certainly the answer I expected.

"Hello, Fi, this is Mike Lusby."

She remembered meeting me at Molly's church, and she had even heard my name before that in connection with the singing that Joe and I did.

"Would you like to go out sometime?" I asked her, bracing for the "no" that was sure to come.

"I think I would like that," she said quietly.

45

I was so shocked that you could have knocked me over with a breath.

For our first date, we went on a singing event with her sisters. We started going out on a regular basis and dated from May until December, about seven months. Then, when I still wondered exactly how she felt about me, she bought me a gray suit for Christmas, something that got my hopes up.

This girl just spent a lot of money on me, I thought to myself. *She must really like me.*

Then, two days later, she broke up with me!

I was devastated. Once I could tell that the break up was definitely going to happen, I remember exactly what I told her.

"Okay, you want to do this? Go ahead. But remember one thing: if you ever want to get back together, you are going to have to come back to me, because I am not going to chase after you."

As much as I liked her, as much as I thought I was in love with her, I just knew I couldn't keep chasing her. Wisdom somehow told me that would only lead to a bad situation. Still, when I left her house that night, I felt completely knocked out.

Now what?

I had started going to her church during that time, so we still saw each other every Sunday, but we didn't talk. Let me tell you this, and it may sound absolutely crazy, but every single night I waited by the phone just wishing she would call. I've told this to numerous people going through painful relationship break-ups and trying to understand where God is leading them.

I started praying, "Dear God, if these feelings I have for her aren't real and they're not supposed to be there, then just take every bit of feeling that I have away. But God, if it is your will for Fi and I to be together, then I pray that every single day these feelings inside of me get stronger and stronger and stronger."

Remaining in God's will was more important than anything else for me at the time. And every day those feelings got stronger and stronger: they wouldn't go away. Every time I saw her my heart ripped out because I wanted to be with her. Those emotions can cause so much pain, and after three months, I grew tired of being alone.

I started dating a girl I'll call Rachel. We went out on a few dates, about three months after Fi broke up with me. But when Rachel and I went out, all I did was talk about Fi. Anyway, Rachel didn't want to go steady, she just wanted to have fun, and I felt okay with that for a time. But one night we walked out to the car.

"You know," I said. "I'm kind of at the place where I think we should either go steady or just break it off all together.

She looked at me for a moment, then said,

"I think I'd like to go steady."

I felt two things in that moment: a small surge of excitement that Rachel wanted to go steady with me and a small twinge of regret, because it felt, in that moment, like anything Fi and I might have had was coming to an end.

I agreed to go steady, and Rachel left. I walked back to the church, thinking through what had happened. But someone waited for me by the door.

"Hey, what's up?" I asked.

"Fi wants to talk to you," she said.

What?!

"Where is she?" I asked, and inside I felt this combination of dread and excitement.

"She's waiting down in the basement of the church."

Walking down those steps, my mind filled with eagerness and worry. I had just told Rachel we should go steady! What could Fi possibly have to say to me?

I found her downstairs and walked up to her.

"I don't know about you," she said, "but I think I'm ready to get back together."

I was in a terrible dilemma, but I played it cool.

"Okay, why don't we just try going out a couple times, see how that goes," I said. I knew exactly what I wanted, but I didn't want to tell her at the time.

That night I called Rachel as soon as I got home and told her I was getting back together with Fi. She was so kind.

"I knew you loved Fi," Rachel said. "She's the only person you ever talk about."

So Fi and I went on a few dates, and I continued to play it cool. Finally, one day I said, in as disinterested a voice as I could muster, "Maybe we should think about getting back together."

It was March of 1975, and she agreed.

What probably hasn't come through in this story so far is how rocky our relationship was, even when we were together. I didn't realize it at the time, but she carried a lot of anger with her over things that had happened in her past, and I still had plenty of rough edges. We fought hard and often. I know today that it was only God that kept us together.

A few months after we started going steady again, I asked her to marry me.

"No," she said. "I'm not ready."

That caught me off guard. I knew that she was the girl I was supposed to marry, but she was still dragging her feet.

I asked her again, maybe a month later. Her reply was the same.

"No, not yet."

Not yet"? What do you mean by "not yet"?

Finally in August of that year, as I left her house one night, she said quietly, "I think I'm ready to let you take care of me for the rest of my life." And that's how she said "yes" to me – not exactly an overwhelming, emotional story, but our relationship in those days was anything but a Hollywood script.

So we got engaged, due to be married in November. I could never have seen the pain that our marriage would bring both of us. I certainly would not have expected our wedding day to be the unhappiest day of Fi's life.

But when you are young, as we were, you tend to cling to the smallest strands of hope. We believed with the fervor of new converts that we were destined to be together, that our marriage was God-ordained, and that our feelings had very little to do with anything.

Then, as the leaves began changing and our wedding day grew closer, something happened that actually made the gulf between us grow even larger and feel more permanent.

Chapter Seven
The Accident

Fi

Mike was such a kind, gentle man. He pursued me as no one else ever had. He loved music, which was something we had in common. His conversion had transformed his life – he lived for God, going to every church service he could and telling everyone he knew about Jesus. Even outside of church he worked hard, and I knew he would make a good husband.

When he first asked me to marry him, I said no. It wasn't that I didn't want to marry him specifically – I didn't want to marry anyone. The whole time we dated, even before he came along, I was so messed up in every sense of the word: spiritually and mentally. But especially emotionally – something didn't work inside of me, something important, something that had to do with responding to love and controlling my anger. I think that because of the abuse I had experienced, even though I didn't remember it, I didn't know how to have good relationships with men. I wanted to have a relationship with a man, but when Mike pursued me, I pushed him away.

One night, I waited for Mike to come pick me up for a date. I sang to myself with excitement while I got ready and then stood in the kitchen waiting for him. I thought about how handsome he was, how kind. I knew we would have a good time. Then the strangest thing happened – as soon as I saw his car coming towards our house up the driveway, I cringed. I didn't want to go out with him. Small bits of panic tried to overwhelm me, but I managed to keep them down.

That's how I felt the entire time we dated: I wanted to be with him, but when I was, or when that time approached, I froze. I couldn't commit to him until he was with someone else. And, like just about everything else in my life, this made me angry.

Yet something inside of me said I should marry Mike. Not "wanted to" or "couldn't wait to," but "should." It's not much to build a marriage on. If a young lady would tell me today that she feels the same way about her fiancé as I felt about Mike, no way in the world would I encourage her to marry him. But that was the choice I made.

Through all of this, he continued to love me, which may have been the main reason I was attracted to him. No matter how I treated him or what I did to him, he continued loving me. I wanted to treat him nicely, and when we weren't together, I resolved to do so. But then we got together, and I didn't know how. Some part of me held back from him, perhaps because I feared being hurt.

I can't tell you how many times I said *no* to his requests for marriage.

"I'm not ready. I'll let you know," I said. That's how we left it. I was so confused.

Then in August of 1975, we got engaged. I can't tell you the date or why I said yes – I don't remember much about the specifics of that year. Something so terrible happened in the coming months that my emotions shut down entirely, leaving me a complete wreck of a person, more lonely and angry than ever before. Worst of all, I decided that emotions of all kinds were far too painful, and I put them in an internal mason jar and screwed the lid on tight.

This is what happened.

In those days, my family no longer lived on the farm – we had moved to a stone house that had a few outbuildings. My father had started yet another business, and I made stone in one of the barns. His new business was masonry, and we had molds of the different stones used to cover the outside of homes, so I mixed the concrete and prepared it to the right consistency. Then we'd fill the molds, let them dry for a few days, and get them ready for my brothers to use on the job sites where they applied the stone.

I drove a Bobcat tractor around one of the barns, one of those small tractors with a scoop in the front. Every few days a load of sand arrived at the back of the barn, and it was always easier if the sand was as close to the mixer as possible. So I used the Bobcat to keep moving the sand forward toward the mixer. It was a small task, just one of the many parts of the process.

That morning, I was doing what I always did: I hopped on the Bobcat and looked around to make sure there weren't any kids in the way. My older brother lived at the end of the lane with his wife and four children; my sister lived half way up the lane with her husband and two kids.

Their youngest daughter was Angie. Nineteen months old, she had springy blond curls and blue eyes and walked like a colt standing up for the first time. She had a lot of personality for a toddler, and many mornings while I worked I saw her walking up to Grandma's house for a treat.

It seemed like kids always ran up and down the driveway or played around the barns, so I was on the lookout for them. Always. There wasn't a time that I climbed up in that tractor without looking around to make sure the kids weren't playing close by.

The morning sky shone crystal clear, not a single cloud, one of those beautiful fall days when the air is crisp and everything seems fine in the world. I climbed up on the Bobcat and picked up a scoop of sand, pushed it forward. I looked around again – no one in sight. I specifically remember staring at the vacant corner, the one the kids often came running around. No one was there. The coast was clear.

Then I backed up, picked up another scoop and pushed that forward. When I turned to look again, I saw her. My 19-month-old niece Angie lay there on the driveway, where the Bobcat tractor had just been.

She still wore her white nightgown and looked like she was sleeping – no blood, no writhing in pain. Just sleeping.

I had backed over her.

Off in the distance, my dad had seen the whole thing take place but couldn't get my attention in time to stop it from happening. He ran to the tractor, picked Angie up in his arms like a baby, and carried her down to my sister's house, half running, half trying not to trip over his grief.

The accident took me into an emotional tailspin. I pulled at my face in horror and opened my mouth. I can't remember if I screamed or if my mouth just opened without any sound. I ran off and hid in the tall grass behind the barn, not crying or screaming, just hugging my knees and rocking back and forth. I squeezed my eyes closed.

This isn't happening. This isn't happening. Soon, I'll wake up, and everyone will be okay. Angie will be okay.

But it wasn't a dream. I heard adults screaming, shouting, and the sound of chaos that flies around unexpected death.

Something about my life always left me feeling slightly alone – maybe it came from being the youngest girl often grouped with three younger brothers; maybe it was my quiet personality; maybe it was a result of the abuse I experienced as a young child. But on that morning, by myself and invisible while all this chaos went on around me, I felt more alone than I had ever felt in my life. I felt like I had been removed from everyone else in the universe.

A hurricane of activity whipped around the farm – my brother's family came running out to see what was wrong. Everyone rushed here and there, wanting to help, but there was nothing to do. Then my sister and my dad drove to the clinic with Angie, stones flying up behind their car as they tore out the drive. Everyone else stayed behind, crying and in complete shock.

In the meantime, I stayed hidden in the grass. What was I supposed to do?

How was I supposed to act?

Is there anyone I can talk to, anyone who can take care of me?

Within the next hour, other family members began arriving at the house. Somehow, I ended up inside. Someone must have come out to the tall grass and retrieved me. I felt so out of touch, in complete shock. Eventually we heard the bad news: Angie was dead. That beautiful little girl, blonde hair and blue eyes, the life of every room she entered, gone at 19-months old.

I couldn't stop wondering if my sister and brother-in-law would forgive me. I think I knew that they would, and they told me several hours later that they did, but in those moments just after the accident, their forgiveness didn't seem like such a sure thing. I had no idea how they would respond.

Later in the day, when they returned from the clinic and came to the house, my mom met them at the door.

"Fi's not doing well," she told them. "She doesn't know if you can forgive her."

They found me in the living room, curled up in the fetal position, hugging my knees to my chest. By that time, my eyes had dried up, like an empty well. They looked so sad, but my sister came over and hugged me, held me tight.

"This wasn't your fault," she said.

I should have felt relieved, I suppose, by her reassurance. I should have eventually felt some kind of upward movement, as if I had gained positive emotional ground. The first step up the mountain. But there was nothing, no movement. I allowed myself to become an emotional shell that nothing, and no one, could penetrate.

Mike had left his work immediately after hearing about the accident and raced to the house. But I don't remember much about him being there. We certainly didn't sit there holding each other, as you might expect an engaged couple to do in a moment like that. His concern for me was real. He loved me deeply. But the accident only served to distance me even further from him.

Our engagement announcement appeared in the local newspaper on the same day as Angie's obituary. My emotional obituary could have been right there beside the story of her short life. It's an old phrase, but for me it was so true: something inside of me died that day. Something turned off, and I either couldn't or wouldn't flip the switch back to the on position.

My relationship with Mike also could have had its own death announcement that day, a few months before we even got married! The accident forced something else in between us – it's not like we were great friends before we got married, with a history of positive emotional experiences. Our relationship was simply "supposed to be," and when Angie's accident took place, it didn't erase the "supposed to be," but it did make me even less interested in becoming Mike's friend. In becoming anyone's friend.

I think back to who I was at that point. I'm so glad that I could not, at that time, see the years of darkness waiting for me.

Chapter Eight
The Saddest Wedding

Mike

When the accident happened and Angie died, I was working at a shop in Wrightsville, about forty-five minutes away. We sandblasted truck frames and did some painting, so that's what I was up to on that morning. Just getting started with my day. I can't remember exactly who called me, but what they said sent a tremor right through me.

"Fi ran over Angie."

Those words shocked me. What do you say to that kind of news?

"I'm quitting work for today," I told my boss. "I have to get home."

So I drove back through morning traffic to Fi's parent's house. When I got there all I saw was chaos — so many folks coming and going, the kitchen bustling as friends and family arrived and figured out what to do about lunch. As I entered the house, some people brought Fi out through the door and what I saw frightened me.

Her eyes darted from spot to spot — she looked like a frightened, wild animal. I felt sure that if those people let go of her arms she would take off running, up into the woods and across the fields and never stop, never look back. She glanced at me with eyes that were not taking in any information — she looked right through me. In another life, she knew who I was, but on that morning, I felt like someone should introduce us.

"Fi, it's me," I said softly. "Are you okay?"

But she walked past me without a word, and she left. They took her to the medical center to get some medication, and I stood there, watching her go, the image of her eyes burned into my brain. She was in shock. A little while after that I left, too, drove to a pay phone and called my mom just to tell her what had happened.

I didn't go back to work for three days — Fi's entire family was together every evening. We sat there in the house and cried and supported each other. Fi seemed outside of it all, above it or perhaps beyond it, in another realm. I'm not sure if she was on medication at that point, but that's how she looked: completely in shock, stuck in a moment inaccessible to anyone else.

The night of the viewing I went with them to the funeral home. We went early, with Fi's sister and her sister's husband and Fi's parents. We parked outside, and the sun hung low in the September sky. I helped Fi out of the car and guided her toward the door. The group of us walked together, Angie's parents at the front. It was a very sad moment.

But as we got closer to the door, Fi did not want to go inside. A small group of us held her close and told her we wouldn't force her to do anything.

"Take your time," we told her. "When you're ready, we'll go in."

She softened, or at least relented.

Eventually, Fi and I went in. As we got close to the coffin and she first saw the body, she let out a wail that shook me to the core.

Little Angie lay there with her eyes closed, as if asleep. Her body looked perfect, not a bruise to be found, and I think all of us fought the urge to shake her, give her a gentle poke, somehow try to wake her up. I remember looking over at Fi in that moment.

A blank look covered her face. She shed very few tears, if any. It was as if all of her emotion exited her body with that last scream and all that remained was a curious bystander. I could somehow tell that massive amounts of pain raged deep inside of her, way under the surface, but none of it found an outlet.

The viewing came and went. The funeral passed, and they buried Angie's tiny body at the same church where I got saved. So much sadness reverberated in our lives during that week, and as we walked away from the graveyard, I found new questions coming up through the grief.

We are supposed to get married in a few months...now what? What's going to happen with this? Fi is not doing well. How is this going to change our relationship?

My mind went a million different directions with that – the truth is our relationship, our dating years were incredibly rocky even before all of this happened. We certainly didn't have the same feelings that most young couples have at that point as they prepare to enter marriage. There was never much of a spark. We disagreed a lot. Fi was controlled by anger, and I was controlled by the fear of what our future might look like.

She's in a different place right now, I thought. *Emotionally, she's devastated. She just ran over her little niece and killed her. Are we going to stay engaged? What's going to happen? What are we going to do with this?*

But true to the normal habits of our generation and community, we didn't talk about it. We certainly didn't go to anyone else for help – that thought didn't even enter my mind. Back then, people only went for counseling after breakdowns or psychological collapses, and even then looking for help wasn't a foregone conclusion.

The months passed, the weeks slipped by, and our wedding day came and went. We got married. But the entire thing happened under a haze of grief and unspoken doubt. What should have been a joyous occasion became, as my wife openly admits, one of the unhappiest days of her life.

If you need proof, just look at our wedding pictures: sadness weighed heavy in her eyes and made smiling nearly impossible. She still grieved little Angie, or wanted to, but I don't think any of us understood grief very well back then, and our background, our generation, demanded a certain façade, a certain toughness. So we stood in front of all of our friends and family and said the old familiar promise: "For better or for worse, for richer, for poorer, in sickness and in health, to love and to cherish; from this day forward until death do us part."

What a solemn promise. "For worse…for poorer…in sickness…:" each of those would be sorely tested in the not-too-distant future.

We never received any counseling or help to get through the issues in front of us. We had more than enough emotional baggage between the two of us, even before Angie died: I had grown up in an alcoholic family, and Fi had unresolved incidents from her own childhood. Yet, we never spoke about any of this. There was no resolution, no progress. In an attempt to cover up our areas of pain and dysfunction, we added layers of complexity: angry outbursts, unexplored grief, and on top of it all, a marriage.

As a counselor, I walk beside people on the dark road of grief all the time, trying to help them understand that the emotional response to an accident like this can take five years or more to process. Intense pain and loss like this cannot be experienced or understood in a few short weeks or months. Yet, we felt the pressure to move on, to move forward, to "trust God."

It was a painful time, and the lack of love Fi felt for me on our wedding day probably only served to remind her of just how far away happiness was at that moment. I didn't kid myself – I knew Fi's lack of excitement wasn't all about Angie's death. I knew better than that. She had some hesitancy about marrying me. In fact, just a few weeks before our wedding day, she dropped this bomb on me:

"If I didn't know it was God's will for me to marry you," she said quietly. "I'd call this whole thing off."

She told me that.

So I knew it was more than grief. But when we were broken up for those three months, I had prayed so passionately, over and over again, the same prayer: "God, if this is not your will, if Fi is not the person I'm supposed to marry, then just take these feelings away." I still believed marrying Fi was the right thing to do.

Thirty-six years later, I still feel that way.

About a week after the wedding, we moved into our apartment, basically half a house. It was a dingy little place, and we barely had any furniture, but it's where we started our life together. Unfortunately, the physical structure and sparse accommodations symbolized the state of our marriage rather well.

One example of this: driving home from work, my thoughts focused on concerns more than happiness.

What kind of mood will Fi be in when I get home? How will she treat me today?

Anxiety gnawed at my gut. She didn't appear to like me very much.

Yet, she worked hard at trying to be a good wife, or at least what she perceived a good wife should be. I left at four in the morning to get to work, and she got up early with me and made breakfast, packed my lunch and saw me off to work. She did all of that, but it was without emotion. I think she did it because she knew it was the right thing to do. That's how she operated for years — whether she felt like it or not, whether the feelings were there or not, she tried to do the right thing.

Married life moved forward in time. There wasn't much laughter. There wasn't any joy.

Sometimes I look back over our situation from the perspective of a counselor. What would I tell a couple who started off in that kind of a situation? How would I attempt to guide them to something better?

Normally, if a married person comes to me and says, "I just don't have the feelings anymore," I ask them a question: Did you ever have the feelings? "Yeah, we had them at one time," they almost always say, to which I respond, "Then you do what you know is the right thing to do, whether you feel like it or not. Make yourself do it. I'm a firm believer that if you do that, eventually those feelings will come back."

If you do things because you know they're the right things to do, the more you do them, the better the chance that it will become your new normal. Then it becomes a way of life to you, and when it becomes a way of life, it becomes easier. People can fall back into love with one another.

But what happens when the feelings were never there? Is it possible to not only work through a painful relationship but to also create something new, something vibrant?

These days, when I work with people, I have to know the entire story in order to help them navigate the troubled waters of their life. Yet in the early days of my own marriage, I definitely didn't know Fi's whole story.

So Fi tried her best. We both did. But at that point it felt very much like a losing battle.

You should know something else about our lives at that time: everything revolved around church. We went Sunday mornings, Sunday nights, and sometimes every night of the week. Our first fifty dates probably involved going to a church. We spent more of our waking time together at church than at home.

Don't get me wrong – church can be a great community and provide much-needed support for couples and marriages. I believe in churches. But in the early days of our marriage, church trumped everything, and I don't think that's right. I don't think church should come before your spouse. Plus, for all the time we spent in church, we continued growing further and further apart.

Eventually, we moved from our small apartment to a 60-foot mobile home on a dairy farm. I worked the farm and Fi helped as much as she could. We loved that place, and while our relational challenges weren't resolved, there was a certain peace that came with working outside. I could tell that Fi enjoyed it, too. But the rocky times still far outweighed the good, and she said something to me one morning that shattered my world and kept me on edge for many, many years.

We sat in our car outside of church. She planned on going somewhere that day, and I probably said something negative to her, discouraging her from going out – my friends find it hard to believe or remember, but I was an extremely negative person back then. I guess she got sick of my negativity.

"I'm tired of this," she said. "I don't want to be married. I can't see myself being married to you for the rest of my life. I want a divorce."

Shock oozed out of every pore in my being. I knew things were bad, but that bad?

That day, when we got back from church, I walked out to one of the meadows to check on something, and

I walked through what was a beautiful day on the farm. A spring sun shone down over that land, and my heart felt broken. Even after all of these years, a small scar remains. I remember crying out to God in the middle of that field.

This can't happen to me! I don't want to be divorced from my wife! I love her, and I always will. I don't want to be a statistic. I have to give it to you, God. I can't do this.

But at that time I didn't realize someone else was in the way. Not only did Fi and I need to overcome our own problems, insecurities, and grief — someone else was trying very hard, and with much success, to wedge his way in between us.

Chapter Nine
The Weight of Guilt

Fi

I don't remember why I agreed to marry Mike. The feelings I had for him confused me more than anything. I didn't say "yes" because I was worried about becoming an old maid, although at 22 years old I was certainly as old or older than most of my friends who were already married. There was just something about him that I couldn't get away from.

But I didn't like him. I really didn't. That sounds so strange and foreign to a lot of people, but it's the truth. I think he knew. I probably loved him as a person, but I had never fallen in love with him in the conventional sense. Yet, we got engaged.

Perhaps it was his kindness that drew me – he was so kind to me, and gentle. I loved that about him. But because of my history, I don't think I could have liked any man. I don't know if it was even possible.

After Angie's death, I tightened up even more towards him. I let other people console me and love me, but when Mike tried to come close to my grief, I clammed up. The only thing I could think to do was run, from everything. I didn't even want him to be at the viewing or the funeral. So why did I go through with the wedding? I guess Angie's death would have given me an excuse to change my mind. But I moved through the haze, and before I knew it, my wedding day arrived.

I felt miserable. On the actual day, I didn't even want to be there. I felt stuck and trapped, as if the final bolt was drawn on my miserable existence. And even though I was surrounded by my loving family, and so many of our close friends, those smiling faces only reminded me of my own unhappiness.

Our pastor married us at the church we had gone to ever since we started dating. A charismatic man, he attracted an enthusiastic congregation willing to do anything for him. We all worked diligently for God at the church; however, our pastor manipulated the entire congregation for his own pleasure.

In fact, what took place during the following years brought me so much pain that I can no longer refer to him as a pastor. Pastors are supposed to lead and guide their flock, caring for them and putting their congregation's needs first. This man did none of these things. From this point on, because it's impossible for me to call him *Pastor,* I'll simply refer to him as *the man, this man,* or *my abuser.*

What no one else knew was that this man manipulated me emotionally and mentally that summer before Angie's death. I worked at the church as a secretary, and he had made subtle advances to me, illicit suggestions just hidden enough that they could be explained away. I told no one – everyone loved this man so much, and I was sure no one would believe me.

This kind of behavior and sexual harassment continued throughout the remainder of that summer as I planned for my wedding. Being chased by the man and planning to marry my man at the same time became more than I could bear. Eventually he suggested casually that we could meet up somewhere.

I stood in his office. He looked up at me from behind his desk.

"I can tell you're hurting. You need to get away for a few days."

At that point I couldn't think of a way to lie to my parents. How could I get away for a few days?

However, the pressure he placed on me was too much, so I went, just for the day instead of for a few days. But I refused to meet his sexual demands. He was very angry with my response, yet smart enough to know that he could not force me to do what I *did not* want to do.

After Mike and I got married, we went to the Poconos for what was supposed to be a four or five day honeymoon, but I was miserable. I hated it. So we came home early, stopping at Messiah College to see some friends who attended there. Who comes home early from their honeymoon? Who interrupts their honeymoon to visit their friends? By Wednesday we were home. And that was just the beginning of my life as Mrs. Lusby.

So much hid inside me, and then Angie's death gave me the perfect cover – everyone believed that my despair, my distress, was solely due to that tragedy. Don't get me wrong – a significant portion of it was because of Angie's death, but so much more of it was simply a lingering depression, a constant feeling of unease and anger that had been with me for a long time, made worse by recent circumstances.

I became a cover-up artist, hiding my emotions, my true feelings. I learned how to hide everything from everyone, including Mike. I spiraled deeper and deeper inside myself, the true Fi nearly vanishing into the darkness.

For the first six months of my marriage, I did what I thought a wife *should* do: I woke up early with Mike, made him breakfast and prepared his lunch. I cleaned the house and washed the dishes and kept everything organized. I followed through on my childhood determination to keep a much cleaner and more organized household than the one I grew up in. Yet happiness eluded me.

I remembered back to my 15-year-old self, lying on my parent's bed, weeping for no discernible reason. *What is wrong with me?* I wondered. Now I know that I suffered from severe depression, but at the time, I didn't know what to do. My parents didn't know what to do with me. I didn't know what to do with myself.

What I didn't realize was that during my growing up years my interactions with men had given me a very confused outlook on life as well as a weak foundation for marriage. The only exposure I had to sexuality and men came in guilt-laden settings that filled me with pain and anger: the homeless man showing me pornographic pictures and being abused as a small child. It was impossible for me to make the transition from how I had been conditioned to view men for so many years (as sexual predators) to now seeing Mike as someone who had my best interests at heart.

I didn't know that the young men who had sexually controlled me when I was four years old had planted a seed deep in my soul that actually made me want to control whatever I could: external things such as a clean house, a clean car, a perfect yard, orderly closets, those kinds of things. It also planted a seed of anger toward men that I was totally unaware of until I was nearly 50 years old.

One Sunday, about six months after we got married, I turned to Mike. We sat in our car in the parking lot before church started. He was probably asking me about something, and, as usual, I got angry. I don't remember the details, but I do remember the hateful words that erupted out of my mouth.

"We're going to end up divorced," I said.

The "d" word. To us, in that church, with our background, it was almost unspeakable. Yet there it was – I had said it. The word hung in the silence like profanity. His eyes immediately filled with pain, something that brought a mixed response in me: on one hand, I felt scared and sad that I would hurt my husband when he tried so hard to be kind and gentle to me. But I quickly realized I had the upper hand, and his response fed the side of me that wanted control.

We covered up our argument and walked into the church, smiling for the moment. But I felt defeated.

Soon after that our pastor approached me again.

"I've left you alone for six months," he said quietly. "But I know you're not happy with Mike. Why don't we meet up again?"

The question was like a punch in the gut, except I knew it was coming. Ever since our previous encounter, something in me had been waiting for him to approach again. I was so desperate for some kind of happiness, any kind of happiness, and my mind had been so twisted and deceived that I thought, *Maybe if I can't find happiness with Mike, I can find happiness with this man.*

As strange as it may sound, I think my earlier, confusing experiences with men and sexuality had somehow programmed me to expect men to be sexual predators, like that man, instead of a gentle, kind man like Mike.

"Okay," I said. "I'll meet you." It was practically a whisper.

And I did.

69

Leaving the man after the first time was like descending into a black hole. I thought I knew guilt before that day – I didn't have a clue. The guilt that descended into my soul made it difficult for me to breathe. It followed me wherever I went, peeked out at me from unexpected corners. From that point on, all I could think about was one question:

"What am I going to tell Mike if he asks me what I did today or where I went?"

But he didn't ask any questions.

I barely remember that summer. Nothing, that is, except the guilt.

That fall the man approached Mike and I to see if we would move to Florida with he and his wife and a select group to work at the church he was going to pastor. It didn't take us long to come to a decision – we needed a change, Mike was excited about getting more involved with church work, and, to be honest, I didn't want the man to leave me behind.

So we agreed to go. We didn't have enough money to make the move because we gave every extra penny we made to that man and our church. In order to move to Florida, we had to sell a lot of our possessions. Then we packed up what was left and headed south in our Datsun station wagon.

Chapter Ten
Watching Her Drive Away

Mike

In those days, before we moved to Florida and while we still lived on that small farm in Cochranville, the first thing I did when I came in from the barns was check the closets. These days when I get home I put the keys on the counter, put away my jacket and take off my shoes, but back then I didn't do any of those things until I had a chance to peek inside the closets.

Why did I do that?

Well, I normally got home from work before Fi, and I had this nagging worry that she would leave me. When I looked inside the closets and saw that her things were still there, I felt a small surge of relief. She hadn't left yet.

But our arguments heated up. They began taking on a predictable pattern – instead of threatening to leave or mentioning divorce, Fi approached it from another angle.

"I wouldn't blame you if you went out and found another woman," she said.

I looked at her through determined, sad eyes.

"I said my marriage vows before God and man, and I'm sticking to them. I am not going anywhere."

Her words confused me – why would she say that? I didn't want any other woman. I only wanted her. Now I know that those words emerged from a guilty heart, a hopeless soul, and a confused mind. But in those days, when she said that, it hurt me to the core.

Then came our pastor's request to join him at the church he was moving to in Miami, Florida. At the time I had grown so tired of farming, exhausted by the seven-day work-weeks, the 70 or 80 hours a week, and moving gave me an opportunity to get out of that. Plus, we both got excited about running a church, starting something new for God. I had begun to feel a call to ministry, so moving South made more and more sense.

As the time for our move grew closer, I looked forward to getting away. A lot of the time I blamed Fi's behavior, unjustly, on her family. *If she wasn't with her family so much, maybe we could get closer,* I reasoned. *Maybe if she detaches a little from her parents and her sisters, our relationship will improve.* But that wasn't the root of the problem, and I think deep down I knew that. Still, the move gave me hope.

We hit the road in our Datsun station wagon, carrying $300 and whatever we could fit in the car. The furniture that we didn't sell, we left in Pennsylvania. The long drive down served to reinforce just how far away we were moving. Neither of us had spent much time outside of Central Pennsylvania, a place saturated with Amish, Mennonites and a very conservative cultural base. It felt like we were getting out into the wide world.

Then, we arrived. We lived in the church apartment, rent-free, for about three weeks, but it wasn't long before we ran out of money. I scrambled all over the city, looking for work in warehouses and restaurants, eventually landing something with a window-blind manufacturer in the city. So I spent my days fashioning shades, and my evenings working at the church. The days were busy, and I put my head down, worked as hard as I could.

Late one afternoon we joined another couple for a game of tennis – they were part of the group that had moved down with us from Pennsylvania. Fi and I stood on one side of the court, batting the ball back to them. We all laughed and had a good time. I watched Fi, and for a moment, I thought back to when we first started dating. I had wanted to marry her so much! How excited I had been when she wanted to get back together after our break-up!

When she ran and laughed like that, it was so easy for me to remember why we were together. Yet, it put a pain in my heart – I wanted that all the time. I wanted that happiness to spread into our marriage and saturate our relationship. I didn't want to only see glimpses of it from time to time.

But during the game, our pastor came driving up on his motorcycle, revving the engine loudly. We were all happy to see him, and we walked over to the edge of the tennis courts and chatted with him while he sat on his bike. We talked about the church and how things had gone for all of us since our move to Miami.

"Hey, you want to go for a ride, Fi?" he asked my wife.

"Sure!" she said, not hesitating.

Before I knew it, the two of them had driven off, vanishing down the road. The other couple hung around and talked for a few minutes. They asked if I liked my job. We discussed more church stuff. Then they left.

I sat at the edge of the court and stared down the street. The hot Miami sun set behind the city, and something inside of me vanished along with it. The air smelled of salt water and a fine layer of sand covered everything – I felt the grit of it under my hands. The streetlights flashed on, and still I sat there, waiting.

Eventually, long after dark, I walked over to our old Datsun and climbed in. I slammed the door closed and sighed, put my hand on the steering wheel and wondered where I had gone wrong. I turned the key, the engine wheezed to life, and I drove back to our apartment by myself.

Walking in, I realized that Fi hadn't returned yet. I checked the closets. Her things were still hanging there.

What in the world is going on? I asked myself. It was the main question on my mind, and it encompassed everything I couldn't understand. What was going on with my wife? What was going on with my marriage? What was going on with this new church?

What was going on with my life?

Chapter Eleven
Running Away

Fi

My relationship with Mike didn't change much after things started happening with that man. I still felt that same old conflict of emotions: excitement at the thought of seeing Mike, but dread and tension the moment he walked into the room. Yet for a very long time, I never imagined actually splitting up from my husband. This confidence didn't always come through in what I said or even how I felt, but certainly in my mind that was how I thought things would play out: we would stay married. At least that's how I felt at first.

But the longer things went on, the more I began to feel the weight of the realization that we would not last like this. We could not. One of us would eventually go crazy, or I'd run off, or Mike would leave me. The man had always dropped hints at the possibility of he and I running away together, and I began to put more and more stock in those "promises." His deceptive words gave me a false hope that, in some ways, helped me to stay put for the time being.

Things will change, I convinced myself. *Someday. Soon. We will run off and get married and…then what?*

But there were times when I still tried so hard to make my relationship with Mike work. For some reason, my dreams refused to disappear: hopes of having a family, and a happy marriage, and contentment. Something inside of me said that if I wanted that, if I truly wanted happiness, it had to be with Mike. So I didn't give up, at least not completely.

Maybe this is why I found myself occasionally saying this to him:

"Some day, Mike, I will be able to treat you like a king."

I wonder what he thought when I said that. I wonder if he found it hard to believe.

Initially when we arrived in Miami, we had no place to live and very little money. We didn't have any work lined up. So we lived in the church parsonage for three weeks before finding an apartment.

Mike found a job in downtown Miami making shades for a large company, and I started working for a Denny's within walking distance, about a mile away. By this time, we were completely broke. We also made payments to a bank in Pennsylvania, but soon we didn't have any money to make those payments. Even after Mike got a job, our financial situation experienced no immediate relief.

"I'm sorry. We have to hold your first paycheck," Mike's boss said, "but I'll loan you any amount of money you need until your first check comes through – then we'll just take a little out of your paycheck each week, whatever amount works for you."

I came home that night, not knowing what his boss had said. It was actually our wedding anniversary, and we didn't have one penny – we couldn't buy food or gas or anything until Mike got his first check.

When I walked into the apartment, I noticed that he had a card on the table still in its envelope.

"What's that?" I asked Mike. He motioned for me to open it.

I pulled back the flap and there were three, $100 bills in there.

I just started shaking. I couldn't imagine where this had come from. It was more money in one place than I had seen in a long time.

"Where did you get this money?" I asked him.

He told me about the arrangement with his boss. I was speechless. It was a miracle.

The nights were hot, and we kept our windows open when we went to bed, sleeping on a mattress on the floor. Sounds from the city echoed through the apartment. I was reading, and Mike came into the bedroom.

He looked at me with a peculiar look on his face, as if he had seen something he'd rather ignore.

"Is there something going on with you and that man?" he asked.

The question shocked me, but I kept a relaxed expression on my face. I looked right into his eyes and didn't even think about the answer.

"No, there's not," I said.

Two years into our marriage, and he was beginning to get suspicious. I was never home when he got home. I treated him poorly. Now, when I think back on those early years, the times that I was giving myself to someone other than my husband, I wonder to myself, *How did I do that? How did Mike survive that? How did he stay sane?* But I think he wanted to believe me, so he did.

We lived there for six or seven months, until July of the following year. Mike hated it in Florida – it was a huge culture shock for him, and our relationship failures were magnified without friends and family around to dull the pain. We had one set of friends that we hung out with, but other than them, we spent time with the man and his wife.

Every day.

Every night.

We hung out with them all the time, and that was something Mike began to resent. The man completely ran our lives, and Mike couldn't wait to get out of there.

It wasn't too long before the church in Miami asked the man to leave, and he decided he wanted to go back to a church in Texas. For some reason, this didn't raise any red flags in our minds. But first, he was going North for a short period of time.

"I want you guys to go to Texas. You can move into a house I have there," he told us one day. "I'm going to be traveling around, and then I'll come down to Texas, and we'll build ourselves a church. But don't get involved in any churches, not until I get there."

So, like dumb sheep, we packed up a moving van and drove to Jacksonville, Texas and waited for him. For a year we floated around, got some jobs and didn't get involved in church. My relationship with my husband continued to deteriorate. Waiting around for the man to return proved difficult.

Then I started to suspect something.

I wasn't the only one.

All of the hope and faith I had put into this man began to evaporate as my suspicions grew – was he seeing other women as well? What would I do? My marriage was dead in the water, and my husband was probably hurt beyond repair. I started to think that perhaps the man who made me believe I was the only one really wasn't planning to run away with me. Could it be?

Any remaining hope leaked quietly from my life. Nothing waited out there in the distance for me to look forward to. There was no one left for me to trust or love. What would I do?

My friend called one day when we lived in Texas. She and her husband had also moved there from the same church we had attended in Pennsylvania.

"Hey, Fi, how's it going?" she asked.

"Good," I said.

She asked me if I could watch her 18-month-old daughter.

"Sure," I said. "Do you want to bring her over here?"

So around lunchtime, she pulled up outside of my house. She met me at the door and handed me her beautiful daughter, almost the same age that Angela was when the accident happened. She told me when she'd be back, but as she walked out I had this sudden realization, something that pierced me to the core and brought me to the lowest point I had ever been.

I stood there holding her little girl and knew, just knew, that my friend was going out to meet up with that man, the same way that I did. I'm not sure how I knew it, but I did. That's why she wanted me to watch her daughter. My knees buckled, and I almost couldn't stand up.

Her little daughter fell asleep on my bed.

I couldn't take it anymore, so I wrote a note to my friend.

I'm sorry that you have come back and I'm not here, but trust me. Please know that I am watching the house to make sure she's okay until you get back. I am leaving. I am going away. I don't know where. But I am watching the house until you come back.

Why didn't I just wait in the house until she got back, hand over her daughter, and then leave? I don't know. Maybe I was scared that I would change my mind. Maybe I didn't want to see my friend again after having had that realization. Maybe I thought Mike would come home and then I'd be stuck, unable to escape. I don't know.

Whatever the reasons, I left the sleeping child, and I parked somewhere, keeping the house within view so that no one would go in to get her. I sat there, a nervous wreck, scared and lonely and wondering what kind of a terrible person would do what I was doing. Then, when I saw my friend's car pull up, and I saw her walk inside, I drove away. I had no idea where I was going – I just needed to go.

I took our little white car. I didn't pack any clothes. Mike had a motorcycle at the time, so I knew he could get to work. I didn't take any money. I drove to Shreveport, Louisiana, about 100 miles away and pulled into a KOA campground. I slept in my car.

I was distraught, confused, tormented, and angry. My mind felt like it had already exploded or was getting dangerously close. Did I just want someone's attention? I wanted help, but who could I ask? Mike, my husband, from whom I was trying to keep the truth? My friend, who I thought might also be involved? I absolutely, positively, could not call the man!

I felt so alone.

Suddenly I felt like I was sitting off in the long grass again, the world racing in orbit around me. I waited for someone to come and put their arms around me and tell me that everything would be okay. That I was forgiven. That they didn't hate me for what I did. But no one came. How could they? No one that loved me knew where I was.

I didn't sleep much that night. The next morning, I woke up having no idea what to do. My back hurt and I felt like a stale mess. I couldn't keep going – I didn't have any money. I couldn't go back to Texas – what would I tell Mike? I couldn't go back home to Pennsylvania – my dad couldn't even imagine one of his daughters having bangs, much less getting a divorce. I didn't have any friends in the bar scene, and I didn't know how to pick anyone up to make some money. And I didn't want to do that.

So I called my friend.

"I'm so sorry," I said. "I just had to get away."

"Fi, where are you?" she sounded concerned.

"I'm not going to tell you."

"Just come home," she begged me. "Just come back."

"I'm not coming back. No way. What am I going to do there?"

"Let me call our pastor," she said. "He'll know what to do."

I shuddered when she mentioned his name, but something in me complied. She called him and gave him my number, and then the public phone rang. I stared at it for a moment, knowing who was waiting on the other end of the line. I didn't want to talk to him, but I had nowhere else to turn. I had no money and felt like I had no other options. What had I been thinking when I left with nothing?

But I desperately wanted someone to talk to. So I lifted the phone out of the cradle.

"Hello?"

It was the man. He convinced me to come back.

Chapter Twelve
God Speaks in the Shower

Mike

When Fi and I first moved to Texas from Florida, we shared a house with another couple that had also made the trek from Pennsylvania to Miami to Texas. They were the ones who had sat with me at the tennis court the day that Fi rode off with our pastor on his motorcycle. Each couple had their own bedroom and bathroom, and we shared the rest of the house. We were good friends, and it was fun living with them.

The four of us basically did whatever our pastor suggested, and he had said we should move to Texas to prepare a church for him, so that's what we did. If I remember correctly, we were there for almost two years before he came down – we spent the time getting to know the area and settling in. But even though he wasn't close by, he still controlled everything.

He didn't want us getting involved in another church. He didn't want us to tell any other preachers why we were there. In fact, one time I made the mistake of mentioning to another pastor what we were doing and that our pastor planned on joining us soon. When we got out to the car, Fi reamed me out. I felt like I had sinned against God by not following the pastor's instructions perfectly.

One day I noticed on the phone bill that Fi was calling our pastor all the time. I mean, all the time.

"If I didn't know any better," I said casually, "I'd think you and our pastor are having an affair."

Her voice came out smooth and relaxed.

"Oh, honey, you don't ever have to worry about that."

Somehow I knew she was lying. I don't know how I knew, but I did. Yet, I couldn't admit it fully to myself. That she might be having an affair remained a remote possibility in my mind, and no matter how the facts lined up, no matter how sure I was that they were together, something inside of me still hoped that I was wrong.

That was the last time that I asked her about it.

Eventually, Fi's two sisters moved down with their husbands. We started gathering our little church together – I studied to become an ordained minister, and after our pastor arrived, he brought me on as his right-hand man, the associate pastor. I was excited to finally be in full-time ministry.

One thing started to bother me, though: my wife was never at home when I got back from work. No matter what time I walked through that front door, she wasn't there. Each time I entered an empty house, my suspicions became stronger and stronger. I usually waited at home for an hour or more before she arrived. It became increasingly difficult for me to listen to the voice that said, "But what if she's not doing anything? Maybe she's innocent."

That voice faded until I could barely hear it.

Finally, I came home one day and reached my limit. I must have had a bad day at work, but when I arrived at the house and she wasn't there, I lost it. The only person I could talk to was God, and he got an earful.

"You know what?" I said. "I'm sick of this. I'm not doing it any longer. I can't live with Fi knowing that she is running around on me! I'm too tired. I'm going into the bathroom and taking a shower, and if she's not here by the time I get out of the shower, I'm packing up and leaving."

I went into the bedroom and got ready to shower. I hadn't given staying much of a chance, seeing that she rarely got home in time for dinner. But as I stepped into the shower, I heard something that surprised me.

The front door closed. Fi was home. She never came home that early. The hot water relaxed my body. Right there, in the shower, I felt God communicating to me as clearly as ever before.

He said, "Mike, if you will let me, I will take care of this for you. Don't give up."

I felt the tears rising to my cheeks, a product of frustration and weariness, but he said it again.

"Mike, if you will let me, I will take care of this for you."

Right then and there, I relaxed.

"Okay, I'll let you take care of it."

After that, I decided I would never question her again. I wouldn't ask her if she was cheating on me or why she treated me the way she did. I wouldn't ask her where she had been or who she spent her time with. Besides, what would I do if she told me the truth?

My way of handling the entire situation would never be perfect – I had no idea what I was supposed to do, what the right thing was to do, or even what I wanted to do. I knew that God could do a much better job of taking care of the situation than I could, so in that area of my life, I sat back and I waited.

Remember the story Fi told about running away to Shreveport? I remember the day she left, coming home to find a note to me on the table. It was the thing I had always feared. I also remember that she came back the next day. But I didn't ask her anything. I didn't ask her where she had gone or what she had done. I acted like nothing had happened.

I knew that God would take care of it.

For the next several years, we focused on building the church's congregation. Our group from Pennsylvania formed the core. We cleared some land and put up the building. For five years, this went on, and during most of that time, I worked at church and had no idea where my wife was. I'd get home, and she'd be gone, and when she got home, she offered no information.

One night, I came home from work to an empty house. Not long after that, my wife arrived with another lady from the church, and they acted like giddy school girls, carrying on and giggling over some kind of inside joke. They reminded me of girls talking about the boys that they liked.

"What were you up to today?" I asked casually.

My wife smiled.

"Oh, Pastor had us running all over the place on errands."

"Really? What for?"

She hesitated.

"He sent us out looking for a lawn mower for the church, stuff like that."

They both giggled again.

"Okay," I said quietly. But I didn't believe a word of it.

Later that evening, I approached Fi.

"I'm going to head over and talk to our pastor about a few things."

So I went over to his house and had a casual conversation with him. As I left his house, I stopped, turned, and asked him a question as if it was an afterthought.

"By the way, do you have any idea where my wife was today?"

He looked me right in my eyes.

"I have no idea. I didn't talk to her at all today."

I acted cool.

"Okay, just wondering."

I got out to my car and sat there quietly, staring at the road in front of me. The night sky hung overhead like a dark blanket. There wasn't a single star to be found.

Now, I know it for sure. My wife is having an affair with this man. What am I supposed to do about it?

But once again, I felt God speaking to me:

"Mike, if you let me, I will take care of this for you."

But God, this isn't right! I know in my heart what's going on! He's a danger to the church, and my marriage is falling apart. Someone needs to find out exactly what he's up to.

"Their sin will find them out."

I sighed, turned on the car, and drove home.

Sometime during 1979, I approached two friends of ours in the church: one was a lady we called Aunt Dorothy, and the other was Debbie. Close friends, they always supported us.

"There's something wrong with my relationship with my wife," I confessed to them. "Can you pray with me for two things? Pray that our marriage is healed, and pray that Fi will want to have children."

Something began to change.

I didn't know it at the time, but this is when Fi pulled away from the other relationship she was in. She spoke to me differently: there was respect and kindness in her voice. But an even bigger miracle happened: suddenly she wanted to have children.

I'll never forget that day she took the home pregnancy kit into the bathroom. She came out, and her hand shook as she held it up for me to see.

"Look at this," she whispered, her voice wavering.

The test read positive. We laughed with tears in our eyes.

"Are you sure?" I asked. "I mean, are you sure you're sure?"

I couldn't believe it. I stared and stared at that little test, and then I couldn't take my eyes off of Fi. Could it be that we were through the worst of it? Would we emerge from the darkness that had enveloped us since before we were even married?

There's one thing for sure – that impending arrival of that little guy brought a lot of joy into our lives, joy that had been postponed and missing and seemingly canceled out. But there it was, staring us in the face as it never had before: joy. Childbirth is a miracle no matter how you look at it, but this was a double miracle because I didn't think my wife would ever want children.

We drove over to tell Aunt Dorothy, and she just laughed. She was so happy for us.

"Look at you two – you're already on your way to look for a crib, and you just found out you're pregnant." She thought that was the funniest thing.

Our marriage changed. Our relationship grew. I could feel something changing in Fi. But we still had never spoken about Pastor or what had gone on for all those years.

At some point during that year, these changes kept taking place in her that I couldn't quite figure out. She seemed kinder, less angry. Then, one night I woke up and realized she was slipping quietly out of our bed and going into the living room. I didn't think anything of it on the first night: maybe she was going to the bathroom or needed a drink. I drifted back to sleep.

But the next night she did the same thing. And the next. Finally, I got so curious about what was going on that I followed her.

I waited a few minutes, until she had been out of the room for a little while. The house slept, quiet and dark – it was the middle of the night. What was she doing, getting up at this time, every night, for that many nights in a row? I took a deep breath and peeked around the corner.

She didn't turn the lights on – I could see that she had a flashlight and was reading her Bible. Later on I found out that she would just sit there and read a verse over and over.

He reached down from on high and took hold of me; he drew me out of deep waters. He rescued me from my powerful enemy, from my foes, who were too strong for me. They confronted me in the day of my disaster, but the LORD was my support. He brought me out into a spacious place; he rescued me because he delighted in me. (Psalm 18:16-19)

The interesting thing about this was that it took place during the time our two friends prayed for her. I didn't realize it, but she had decided to work hard at doing the right thing.

December 3rd, 1981 is a date I will never forget.

The denomination of which our church was part held a Christmas party, and all the churches in our area got together. There was a lot of talking and laughter with Christmas music playing in the background. Fi was seven months pregnant, and we couldn't wait to be parents. For some reason, Fi left the party before I did.

Then a guy from our church came up to me, a good friend. He had a strange look on his face, as if someone he liked and admired had walked up to him and punched him for no reason. His countenance certainly didn't fit a Christmas party.

"Hey, what's wrong?" I asked. When he spoke, it was as if he was talking in his sleep.

"Pastor's wife is on a rampage," he said, looking around to make sure no one else listened. "Apparently, he has a lot of women on a string in our church. He's been having sex with them."

My heart sank, and I felt a numb sensation spread throughout my body. Part of me wanted to walk away and forget what he said. But the rest of me felt released in a way that only happens when you hear the truth you have suspected for a long time.

He paused, then said words that didn't come out easily.

"My wife was one of them."

I stared at him, shocked. But not surprised. Does that make sense? All those years, I wondered if something was up with our pastor, but my "better" judgment said it was impossible. My mind raced a million miles a minute. *A lot of women,* he had just said, *on a string.* I took a deep breath, only able to gather the strength to ask one question.

"Was Fi one of them?"

"I'll call you tomorrow," he said.

I went home and found Fi in bed, already asleep. I crawled in under the covers beside her and didn't say a word. I'm not sure if I slept at all that night, or if I just lay there, staring into the darkness, until the morning sun rose. Looking back now, it was very much like the night I spent staring at the ceiling after Donnie asked me that question. Only on this night I didn't feel like I had anywhere to go when I woke up.

The next day at work, I sat at my desk in my office, meeting with someone. Then, the guy from the Christmas party called.

I don't remember much about our conversation other than one sentence that he said: "Fi was one of them."

I hung up the phone, and the gentleman in my office looked concerned.

89

"Are you feeling okay?" he asked. "You just went white as a sheet."

All the blood had drained from my face, and I felt like I might pass out. You think you know something, but until you hear it with your own ears from a third party, it never sinks in. When I heard verification of the one thing I had feared all those years, it devastated me.

For a week, I walked around work like a walking dead man. Even though I had always known in my heart what was going on, when I finally found out for sure, it killed me. It ripped my heart out. All the pain I had kept at bay with the thought, "Maybe it's not true," came rushing in as soon as the fact was confirmed.

The next day, the pastor vanished. He called me because I was the associate pastor.

"You tell me," I practically shouted at him. "What am I supposed to do with this church?"

Instead of feeling sorry or embarrassed, he got mad.

"You people think I can't do anything that I want? I'll come back to that church. I'll do my dirty work again, and I'll cover it up like a cat."

I preached for a few weeks before the board appointed his son as the head pastor. Eventually everything went back to being like it always had.

When Fi found out that I knew, a few days after December 3rd, she came to me with sadness on her face that was the result of a lifetime of disappointment, anger, despair and hopelessness. It was hard to see her that way — by then we had nearly two years of an improving marriage behind us. She had worked hard to be a better wife, and I had tried my best to love her more than ever. Not only that, we were about to have our first son. I don't know what she expected me to say, but she came to me anyway.

"Can you ever forgive me for what I did?" she asked, looking devastated, perhaps preparing for the worst.

"I already have," I said. The kindness and determination that I heard in my own voice surprised even me.

Forgiveness is a powerful thing to experience. Forgiving Fi came relatively easy – she was my wife, pregnant with my son, and I had such a strong desire to make our marriage work. But forgiveness doesn't always come easy. Forgiving the pastor who hurt us so horribly was a longer process.

I remember waking up in those days shortly after finding out about what had been going on between Fi and our pastor, and I felt like I had two options. I could buy a gun and some bullets, find him, and shoot him. I'm serious – that's how angry I was. I contemplated this option for a long time.

Or I could make a choice to forgive him. To walk away and release him to whatever fate would be his. This seemed less fair than option one, but it also meant I wouldn't end up in prison for the rest of my life.

God, out of those two options, I know the one I should take. I know I should forgive him. I am going to forgive this man for what he did to my wife and to me.

The process of forgiveness involves, first and foremost, making the choice to forgive. When we make that choice, the process of forgiveness begins, in that moment. It's a powerful point in your personal timeline. But it doesn't mean you will wake up the next morning feeling that things have been resolved, or that life is perfect, or completely forgetting about what happened.

I made a decision to forgive that man, and the process began in me in that moment, but I still woke up the next day and wanted to rip his head off. But then I had to remind myself, *Remember, Mike, yesterday you made the decision to forgive him. So let it go.* So I let it go. I had to do that day after day, week after week, and month after month.

I reminded myself that I forgave him every morning when I woke up.

Then one day around lunchtime, it suddenly hit me: I hadn't thought about him all morning. That was the first time that had happened – every other morning I woke up overwhelmed with hate and anger.

The process of forgiveness must be completing itself, I thought to myself.

Soon, I found myself able to feel sorry for the man and the life that he had created for himself, the path of destruction in which he lived. God even gave me the ability to pray for his soul. Jesus came that ALL might be saved, and it saddened me to think that he would end up spending eternity in hell if he didn't turn to God.

It's not "forgive and forget." Forgive and forget doesn't exist in a case such as this, or at least not in my experience. 29 years later I still think about what happened to my wife and I. I haven't forgotten. But it doesn't bring me all the anger and anxiety that it brought me back then. In fact, when I remember those events, they now remind me of God's goodness, his faithfulness, and the way that He can redeem any situation.

Chapter Thirteen
I Want Out

Fi

In the fall of 1980, about a year and a half before the Christmas party where Mike found out about that man, I sat in my house, staring at myself in the mirror. My face looked drawn and thin, stressed. *Who is this person?* I wondered. *Who have I become?*

I was 27 years old, but I felt much, much older. Guilt had become a way of life – when I woke up, it was there. When I went to sleep, it was the last thing I thought about. Every time I looked at Mike, I felt it. Every once in a great while, I would still tell Mike something that I hoped would one day come true.

"Some day, I am going to treat you like a king."

I wonder what he thought when I said that? I wonder if he believed it could ever happen?

Yet in the fall of 1980, deeper inside of me than even the layers of guilt, something strange and beautiful appeared. I was beginning to feel like I might want a baby. I never felt that before – in fact, I was very opposed to it, and I always told Mike that was never going to happen.

But, God.

Mike and I had connected with a wonderful couple at our church. We started hanging out with them a lot, and they became a tremendous influence in our lives, showing us exactly what a Christian marriage could look like. I watched them, still in the throes of my other relationship, but I began to see and desire what they had. The way they had fun together. The way they treated each other with respect and love. The mutual admiration.

I wanted all of those things with Mike, and I felt like God was beginning to soften my heart. Even if it was just a tiny, tiny bit. God was giving me a determination to change the path my life had taken. I knew it was time to leave that other man for good, but I also knew there would be a price to pay if I ended this craziness.

After all, he had always said, "There's no way you'll ever get out of this relationship. What we have going on is just too good. You wouldn't have the will power to leave me."

I never felt worried for my safety, but I knew that he would try to take every advantage of his emotional grip on me and that he would do his best to cause me a lot of pain if I left. I knew how he would respond. Plus, my husband was the associate pastor under this man – would he fire Mike? Would he make his life miserable? Would he tell Mike what had been going on?

But in spite of all this confusion, I kept thinking about how to leave, becoming desperate to get out from under this guilt and condemnation. Our friends continued to show us what a good marriage looked like, and I wanted that. My desire for children grew stronger and stronger. I knew the journey toward wholeness and healing would be long and hard, but I was ready.

So the next time I saw the man, I told him.

"This is it! It's over! I can't do this anymore!"

At first, he just laughed. He didn't think I could keep my resolve to leave. But when he saw just how serious I was, he got furious. I wasn't sure what he would do. Finally, he turned and looked at me.

"You're a lesbian. You're leaving me for another woman, aren't you! I can't believe this! Fi, that's disgusting and immoral. How can you do this to me?"

How could HE accuse me of being immoral? I thought.

I was totally taken aback. I realized at that moment this was the kind of emotional manipulation he had used on me for the last five years.

'That's not true! It's just not true! I just can't do this anymore. I want a real marriage – I want to make it work with Mike."

My response angered him, and he kept berating me, going on and on about how I would regret this decision.

"I know why you're getting out of this relationship. If you were leaving me for your husband, I could deal with that. I'd still be angry. But leaving me for a woman? What is wrong with you? I always knew your mind was twisted."

"You won't last," he said. "You'll be back."

During the days and weeks that followed, he tried his best. He'd show up at the house when he knew I'd be there alone. He threatened me constantly.

"You'll never get away from me," he said. "I'll never stop."

The very thing I had feared came upon me, and at that moment, I knew it would be far more difficult than I had ever imagined. I walked through this experience all by myself. I didn't tell anyone. I didn't want anyone else to know.

I went through the winter, enduring his harassment. The determination to be a good wife grew inside of me, and I knew I had to do an about-face.

As winter turned into spring, I found myself thinking a lot about having children. I decided it was time to tell Mike the good news. I was ready to be a wife *and* a mother. We both knew that having children wouldn't solve all of our problems, but we also knew a child would bring us a lot of joy. God knew exactly what we needed at that time in our lives. His perfect timing is incredible.

When I got pregnant, that was one of the happiest days of my life. Something about that life growing inside of me represented a fresh start, a clean slate, and in some ways that's how I felt.

One day I drove to a prenatal doctor's appointment. The sun shone, and the world seemed new — I loved being pregnant, loved everything about it. I never felt sick or off in any way — just healthy and energized and determined to follow through on my new life. But as I drove, I saw a car come up behind me, then pull alongside me on the highway. The driver waved me over to the shoulder, and I saw it was the man. Instantly, fear gripped me and I wondered, *How does he know where I am?*

I can still picture the place. I pulled over, and his car rolled to a stop in front of me. He came back and got in the passenger's side, and he began talking. At that moment, I thought, *Why did I stop?*

But then instantly, I knew the answer.

I was afraid.

"What are you doing? How did you know where I was going?" I asked him.

"That doesn't matter. What matters is you can't leave me."

The color drained out of my face, both from panic and anger. Would he never stop with this?

"I made my decision. I'm not coming back! I'm pregnant, and I'm happy with my husband."

I was so angry that I wanted to spit in his face. He paused, scrambling for words.

"You can't be happy. I'll make sure of it."

Eventually I drove away, shaking. His constant harassment continued to wear down on me, but I never went back to him. Mike and I were going to have a baby. Life held a real, tangible promise for me. I was not going to jeopardize that.

When my son was born, it was like God smiled down on me. On us. I had this overwhelming sense that everything was going to be okay, and I realized for the first time that God could make all things new.

The recovery process for Mike and I was not regimented. I can't point back and say, "First we did this, then we did that, and finally, after we did all of these things, our marriage was better and I felt completely recovered." It just wasn't that way for us.

We did start to get some counseling, and that helped our marriage immensely. We probably should have gone to counseling much longer than we did.

But if there's anything that I started to do on a consistent basis, it was listening to the still, small voice inside of me and trying hard to do what I knew was right. For all of those years I had ignored that voice, never listening when it told me to leave the man or to treat Mike better. When I started listening to what I knew was the right thing to do, in whatever situation, my entire life began to change.

We also discovered that two other couples had much the same experience as we had with the man. The six of us spent long evenings together – this became our therapy, although we didn't know it and didn't call it that at the time. To us, it just became a refreshing time of honesty and truth. We needed to debrief. We needed to talk about what we had been through, and that small

97

group provided all of us with a safe place to remember things, get them out in the open, and then move on.

The difficult part for me, and what continues to be a challenge, was that even after talking through much of what had happened, I still held on to so many unresolved, unspoken hurts from my past. What about Angie's death? I had never mourned her loss properly or allowed myself to have any emotion. What about being shown pornography as a child? This had a huge impact on me, but I had never told anyone about it. What about my ongoing bouts with depression, anxiety, and anger? These things were not going to simply vanish, leaving me to live the wonderful life finally mapped out in front of me.

There were still so many things for me to learn — about Mike, about life, and especially about myself.

Chapter Fourteen
Moving Home

Mike

When I look back on my life during our days in Texas, much of it is a roller coaster. When Fi started to change and she wanted to have children, an unexpected happiness invaded my life. Then, when she showed me the positive pregnancy test, her hands shaking, I was up on cloud nine.

I walked around like a zombie when I found out about the affair, about as low as I would ever get. But it's amazing how sometimes things need to come out and we need to hit bottom, before we can make any real progress, before our lives can turn around and we can find happiness.

The most important thing I learned throughout all of this is that God is no respecter of persons. It doesn't matter how important or rich you are, or what kind of a life you have lived. His grace is enough. He hears your prayers. The things he did for us and our marriage, he can do for everyone.

I often started things without ever finishing them. I quit school when I was 16 (although I did recently obtain my GED). I felt this bad habit sort of infiltrating my life, where I would get excited about something, start it, and then never finish it.

When we first moved to Texas, our denomination had something they called Youth Reps. These people were overseers for the youth pastors, and they planned a monthly meeting for all the youth in the section. Every year, they voted in a new Youth Rep – for some reason, during one year that I was in this meeting, I got voted in as the Youth Rep. But I wasn't credentialed at the time.

"We know you're going to get your credentials," my boss said, "so we'll let you go ahead and take the position."

Uh-oh.

But it motivated me and gave me something to work towards. I took correspondence courses and passed them. Then I had to take an eight-hour test at one of the churches in our District, and all of the District leaders were there. I took a written test and a verbal test – the latter meant sitting down with some of the denominational leaders and answering any question they threw at me.

I was pretty ignorant of the Bible in those days, especially the Christian jargon. After all, I grew up outside the church and hadn't been introduced to the Bible until my late teens. But I studied hard. A memory flashed through my mind, and I pictured my father, the way he always used to look when he said:

"You'll never amount to anything."

So I worked hard, I finished that test, and I passed.

From Jacksonville, Texas, we moved to Austin. Fi's sister and her husband had found a great church there, so we joined them. Our friendships there helped continue the healing process for us and gave us a chance to rebuild our family relationships and work through some of the extremely difficult times we had experienced.

The only problem with our new church was that the pastor reminded me so much of our old pastor, the one who had caused all the trouble. It took me a long time to work up the courage to talk to him, but eventually I decided to be honest.

"I've been hurt, and I don't like preachers," I told him one day over lunch.

We told them our story, wanting to be transparent, but also worrying that they might ask us to leave or treat us differently once they heard about our lives. But they loved us. They treated us so well, with immense respect and kindness. It put another boost of energy behind our determination to make the most of the heights to which God had brought our marriage to.

It probably took me about six months to start feeling comfortable at the church. I realized the pastor was genuine and his love for God was real. He knew us and he knew our stories, yet he still loved us and wanted to be our friend. We ended up spending a lot of time with the pastor and his wife – we'd often go out to eat after church.

The love of God.

That's what brought healing to us – God's love displayed through his people.

Then another blessing: Fi got pregnant again. The morning our second son was born, Fi had stayed home, heavily pregnant, and I went to church to help set up for Sunday School. I walked through the building, thankful for where God was taking us.

Then, a friend came up to me.

101

"Your wife is trying to reach you," he said. "She's on her way to the hospital — the baby is coming!"

"What!" I immediately started rushing around, trying to figure out what to do.

"Are you going to the hospital?" he asked me.

"Yes! Yes. Go to the hospital." I paused. "Where's the hospital?"

We hadn't been in Austin long, and I had no idea where the hospital was. He agreed to drive me there, and at about five minutes after twelve, our second son arrived in the world.

When our second son arrived, he was yet another reminder of how much our lives had changed. After the nurses weighed him and wrapped him in a blanket, I carried him from the delivery room to the nursery. He felt so small in my arms, so alive.

Joy overwhelmed me. If anyone had spoken to me, I would have burst into tears of happiness.

Other issues still battled inside of me — my calling as a pastor, for example. I often thought back to the promise I made to God when I was a boy: "God, if you help me out of this mess, I will spend the rest of my life helping people out of their messes." I was in contracting at the time, working as a painter, and I was pretty sure that "helping people out of their messes" didn't involve painting their kitchen.

I continued meeting with the presbyter within my denomination, even though I wasn't preaching at the time. I told him how much I couldn't stand pastors anymore — after what had happened to Fi, most of them just gave me the creeps.

"For every bad preacher," he cautioned me, "there are 100 good ones."

"That's easy for you to say. And to be honest, right now I don't believe it."

But our pastor in Austin helped me to begin to accept that statement. In the meantime, I worked for a painting contractor for maybe six months, then started working for Fi's brother who had also moved to Texas. I built sheds with him. And at first it was a relief to be out of pastoring. I didn't care one way or the other if I ever got back into the ministry. I wanted to get as far away from it as I could.

Then, one day when I was building sheds, I started talking to God.

Will I ever get back into the ministry? This is okay, this is a living, but building sheds is not the deal we had. It's not what you've called me to do. You've gotten me out of mess after mess, and I'm ready to start helping others.

I began to understand something: God had allowed me to step back from my calling for a time, so that I could heal. God let me go away for a little while, but all those days while I was building sheds, I knew it wasn't forever. I knew that he would call me back sometime soon.

This is such an important concept – sometimes God leads us into seasons of rest. He wants to remove us from the thick of the battle so that we can heal and recover. Fi and I needed a time like this in the worst way. But that is never a permanent place – it's never a place to set up residence. I began to feel deep inside of me that a call back into the ministry was not too far in the future.

During one of our trips up to Pennsylvania to visit family, we met up with a friend who was now the pastor of our old church.

"Would you ever consider coming back to Pennsylvania to build a church in the West Chester area?"

Fi and I talked about it a lot during the following weeks. We discussed moving home, having the kids around their grandparents, and being back in the area where we grew up. So after a lot of prayer and consideration, we decided to do it.

We would move back to Pennsylvania.

I would be a pastor again.

As it worked out, Fi's two sisters and their families also moved north with us. We came back in this huge caravan of cars and vans and trailers and stuff tied to everything. We arrived at Fi's mom's house and just about everyone was there – those who had been part of the caravan, plus all of our family members who lived in Pennsylvania.

I sat out on the deck that night with one of my brother-in-law's who had also made the move up from Texas with us. We didn't say much, just sat there looking out over the cornfields as the sun set. The caravan of cars remained in the driveway, not even unpacked.

I had grown to love Texas, in spite of all the bad things that had taken place down there. It had become home for me, the place our life had turned around, the location where God had reached down and snatched us out of a nightmare. It was the place that both of my boys were born. For a moment, doubt entered my mind: Why had we left Texas?

I turned to my brother-in-law.

"What in the world did we just do?"

Chapter Fifteen
Rediscovering My Emotions

Fi

After everything with my abuser had come out, and Mike and I had our two sons who brought us so much joy, it was easy to think that was it – I was back in control of my life. Things were good. All of my issues were resolved.

But that wasn't the case. After we moved back to Pennsylvania and started our church in West Chester, I realized that something inside of me still didn't make sense. There were too many layers for me to break through in one event – getting my marriage right wasn't going to solve every emotional problem that had built up during my life. As much as I wanted to get on with things, there was still work to be done. My path towards healing was in its infancy.

By the time 1989 rolled around, I felt exhausted. Worse than that, I began to see that I didn't experience life like most people I knew. I saw my friends experience happiness or sadness, joyful with life or weeping at a funeral, and I realized that I had a problem: my emotions were dead. I started to feel dead.

One day, while spending time with a friend of ours from the church, a professional counselor, she looked at me, her head tilted to the side, and she told me the first of many revelations that I needed to hear:

"You are angry," she said.

"What?! What are you talking about?" I asked, almost laughing. "I'm not an angry person!"

"No, you certainly don't act like you are an angry person. It's not that you show it all the time. But somewhere inside of you there is a lot of anger."

She didn't press the issue, but her words stirred something in me, a curiosity perhaps. I knew anger was the only emotion I felt capable of expressing – the others simply weren't there. I believed something must be wrong with how I processed emotions. After that eye-opening moment, I went to another close friend and explained to her how I felt.

"Something is going on inside of you," she confirmed to me. "There's something in there that you need to uncover."

Not long after receiving that revelation, I began to recognize that anger lived in me, a simmering rage I couldn't understand. I hated how it seemed to only show itself to the ones that I loved.

Here's an example. As my son prepared for school one morning, he pushed my buttons one too many times. I can't even remember what we argued about, but in my anger, I grabbed him by the back of the neck, with force. The instant I did it, I let go – my own anger shocked me. After he got on the bus, I ran back to my bedroom and wept bitterly, realizing for the first time just how angry I was. It scared me.

The question I asked myself was, *How could I do that to someone I loved so deeply?*

From that moment on, I better understood how people can actually hurt their children – we are a nation so full of rage, and if we don't recognize it and do something about it, that build-up of anger explodes in unexpected fits of violence. In that moment I knew that I had to get help. I contacted Dr. Dobbins, a counselor and close friend of my sister and brother-in-law, to line up a meeting. Mike and I drove out to Ohio to see him.

When we first got there, he talked to me for a long time. I told him my entire life story or at least the parts that I thought might be important as we tried to find the source of this anger. But something remarkable happened: as I walked him through my life story, not once did I get emotional about anything. I didn't feel anger towards my abuser; I didn't feel sadness when talking about Angie's death; I didn't feel regret or happiness about leaving Texas.

Nothing.

Dr. Dobbins instructed me to write down the story of Angie's death.

"Just tell me about that one incident," he said.

Lord, please let me feel the accident. I want to feel the pain. I want to feel something.

I knew that moment, Angela's death, held a lot of significance for me, because that is when my feelings completely shut down. So I wrote out the story as best as I could, and I gave it to Dr. Dobbins.

He looked up at me with kind eyes after reading my story.

"Fi, if I read this and didn't know who wrote it, I would think that it had been written by a neutral observer. It's like a completely factual news article – there is just no emotional pull anywhere."

"I know," I said. "That's how I felt when I wrote it."

After a few more sessions, it was time for us to go home, and I still hadn't experienced the breakthrough I so desperately wanted. When we got home, I visited

Angie's grave. I sat by the headstone and thought back to that day and everything that had happened since.

But I couldn't tap into any emotion.

A few months later, I started meeting with another therapist. We talked a lot, and she's the first person who brought up abuse.

"While I can't pinpoint exactly what's going on with you, Fi, I would have to say that you have all the classical symptoms of someone who was abused as a child."

I told her about the various sexual abuses I had encountered.

"But nothing when I was a child," I said. "At least nothing that I can remember." This was before I received that phone call in 1997.

We started doing some therapy designed to take me back to my childhood in the hopes of unearthing some memories that I had perhaps forgotten, but nothing came up in those sessions.

So I enrolled in group therapy with five other women. One by one, we told our stories, everything that had happened to us. As each woman told her story, they wept and often had to stop to regain composure.

Yet I rattled off my story without shedding a tear. I talked about my childhood, my anger, my engagement to a man I didn't like. I told them about Angie's death and my unhappy wedding day and everything that happened with my abuser. I made it through my entire life story without getting emotional or shedding a tear. That really bothered me.

Then came that phone call at my mom's house around Christmas where the man who had lived in my neighborhood admitted that he and two others had sexually abused me when I was four years old. It was as if, before he called, I had been working on a 1000-piece puzzle of my life and had nearly finished it. Except there was still one piece missing.

The information he gave me completed the puzzle. *There it is. There's my missing piece.*

Shortly after that, he and his wife came to our house. He wanted to apologize to me in person – it all made me very nervous. However, I had some questions, and Mike and I thought it would be best to work through it instead of avoiding it.

They walked into the house, and we shook hands. Small talk: the weather, Christmas, family stuff. We sat down in the living room. How do you begin a conversation such as that?

"I feel horrible," he began. "But I had to tell you. I couldn't live with this guilt any longer. I came to say I'm sorry, and I ask for your forgiveness."

We talked about the event for a few minutes before I asked him some questions.

"Did I fight?" I asked.

He looked at the floor for a moment, and when he spoke, his voice was unsteady.

"Fi, you fought as much as any little four-year-old girl could fight."

Oh, my, I thought. *This is where all of my anger has come from. This is why I am such an angry person.*

"You fought with everything inside of you," he said.

I pictured myself, a four-year-old girl on a barn floor, fighting as hard as I could in the dust and the dirt and the hay, against three teenage boys.

After they left, I sat quietly in my chair. I had no idea that the event had ever occurred, no memory of being abused by those boys at such a young age. But his story helped me make sense of my life. This is why anger had haunted me for as long as I could remember: being abused, being shown pornography when I was 13, the pain that I felt when daddy would vanish, Angie's death. So few details of my life remained in my mind – I think I just learned from an early age how much easier it is to block life out.

A sense of rejection has begun to make itself known to me. I know now that I must have felt tremendous rejection and guilt as a child after being abused. Little by little, moments arrive seemingly out of nowhere, and I will feel something. Most times I don't know what it is that I'm feeling.

But I do know that you cannot stuff your emotions and be healthy. No matter how painful it might be to allow yourself to feel, you must go there. Without emotions, you will feel dead and disconnected. You will ask yourself the same question over and over again.

What is wrong with me?

In the fall of 2010, I was with my sister Anne at a conference. She leaned over to me at one point and asked me to share about Angie's death and how I felt when it happened. Periodically, she would ask me to do this at various events, and I never knew exactly what to say.

As I stood in front of the crowd and began to share about that day, I felt an emotion. It began in the gut of my stomach and pushed its way up and slowly unscrewed the lid. For the very first time in over thirty long years, I had a feeling that I could identify, and it overwhelmed me. I wept, unable to speak.

I realized that feeling was loneliness.

Immediately, my mind went back to the moment when I sat in the tall grass right after the accident.

Where was everyone?

No one had been with me, and there had been no one around. I had felt so alone. I don't know how long I sat there quietly in the tall grass after Angie died. Five minutes? Fifteen minutes?

Tears streamed down my face as the emotion of loneliness washed over me. But I also felt a surprising sense of joy.

I have emotions! I can feel! I am alive!

Each of these revelations about myself played a key part in my healing process. As I continue on my journey toward wholeness, God has given me truths over and over again that have sustained me and encouraged me to press on.

There is a quote from my pastor that I've thought about many, many times:
God sees the tears in our hearts that never reach our eyes.
It gives me peace and assurance that God understands my journey and will continue to walk beside me in my search for emotional healing.

I also read something about how God will take the bad things that happen in our lives, the disappointments and discouraging events, the pain and the misery, mix them all together, and bring about results that someday we will love.

I believe this.

There is a portion of scripture that describes exactly what God did for me in my life:

He reached down from on high and took hold of me; he drew me out of deep waters. He rescued me from my powerful enemy, from my foes, who were too strong for me. They confronted me in the day of my disaster, but the LORD was my support. He brought me out into a spacious place; he rescued me because he delighted in me.

(Psalm 18:16-19)

I love the visual in my mind of being in a spacious place. I picture myself in a field of yellow daisies, running with my hands raised towards the Heavens. I can feel the grass under my feet, and the sky stretches out forever all around me. There's a light, warm breeze blowing. Nothing in the world can intrude on that place. There's freedom and joy and peace. And in that moment, in that spacious place, I remember.

God rescued me.

111

Chapter Sixteen
Two Funerals and a Wedding

Mike

I got that call on June 19th, 1991, at three a.m. on a Friday morning. Woke me out of a dead sleep. In a few hours I would normally be up and going to work at the market stand we owned. I also pastored a church in those days.

I answered the phone in the dark. It was my mom, and immediately I wondered, *Why is my mother calling me at this time of night?*

"I have some bad news for you," she said. No emotion, no tears, just the words.

"Oh, really." I said, more of a statement than a question. I felt sure it had to do with my dad. He had been sick for a long time and was actually in the hospital recovering from a lung operation.

I was not ready for what she said.

"Sonny was killed in a car wreck."

My brother was dead.

I wept like a baby for a long time. I think mainly because the last time I had spoken with him, we had talked about Jesus.

"Mike," he had said in no uncertain terms. "You live your life the way you want to live your life, and I'll live my life the way I want to live mine."

Those words sounded familiar. I remembered saying almost the exact same thing to Donnie or his wife when they asked me if I'd go to church with them. His reply took me back to that time.

My first reaction to the news of his death was the worry that he went to hell. I still don't know whether that is the case. The only hope that I have is that his wreck took place right outside the house of a Christian guy that I know. Sonny lived for fifteen minutes after the accident. This Christian went out and took hold of his hand and started talking to him as he passed.

That's my hope.

But at first, I didn't know any of that. I felt so much pain after Sonny's death that I began shutting down my emotions. From that point, for an entire year, I preached every Sunday without feeling anything. I couldn't feel God anywhere.

I think I was angry, I really do. Because years ago, soon after I became a Christian, I had this vision of all of my brothers and sisters lined up at an altar giving their hearts and minds to Jesus. So when Sonny died, apparently without finding Christ, I got angry.

God, what about that vision? What about that promise?

For that entire year, I lived my life strictly based on what the Word of God said. I still believed it, but I didn't feel any emotion when I read it. I didn't have any feelings of God being anywhere near me; in fact, I felt that he was as far away as the East is from the West.

But I dedicated myself to following it. This is the advice that I give to people today when they encounter a huge loss or plunge into grief: keep doing what you know is right. Don't get sidetracked by a lack of feelings or emotion. Eventually life will come back around, and you'll be glad that in the interim you didn't do something that ruins the rest of your life. Plus, doing the right thing when you don't feel like it is one of the best ways to find recovery.

Something else that I realize now that I didn't realize then is that often an unexpected loss like that can take five years or more to grieve and work through. My brother Sonny and I were as close as two peas in a pod – we were eight years apart, but he drove me all over the place when I was a boy. He took me to his friends' houses or out singing. He took me to the movies and the diner. I was with him a lot.

When he died, he was only 48 years old.

I got stuck in a grieving process.

It's hard to tell how this affected Fi and I. When we first moved to West Chester, she did not want to be there. She was still living under a lot of guilt and condemnation from what had happened earlier in her life. We had these two little boys, ages nine and six. So I'm not sure how this event affected our relationship – there was so much going on at the time.

Then, my dad died in 1999.

He and my mom worked for my wife and I once a week at a retail store that we owned. They didn't have jobs at the time, so he came down and helped us with some of the things that needed to be done. He started to really struggle physically – sometimes by the time he walked from his car to our store, he could barely breathe.

"Dad, you don't need to be here. Why don't you just go home?"

So he'd go home and rest.

He got sick and went into the hospital, and he spent two weeks there while they tried to discover the problem. Finally they sent him in to Lancaster General

Hospital for a heart catheterization, but his arteries wouldn't give way. They couldn't get the heart catheter through.

That night I sat in the room with my mom and my sister. At one point he looked at me with weariness all over his face.

"Son, I can't hang on any longer."

I stared at him, my dad, lying there. He had changed so much from the father I knew as a kid. He wasn't a mean, violent alcoholic anymore – he was a wonderful grandfather to my two boys and an excellent husband to my mother. In fact, I think my sons found his past very hard to believe when they were old enough to hear about my childhood.

"Promise me," he said, "that you won't put Mom in a home when she gets older."

"We can promise that," I said. I realized that he held on for her. He still felt responsible for her, even when his body couldn't do it anymore.

"Honestly," he said again. "I just can't hang on any longer."

When I got home that night, I looked at Fi and said, "I'll be surprised if he makes it through the night."

The next morning, I went to the store, and around 9:00am, I got the call. They didn't tell me that he had died, only that I needed to get to the hospital. By the time I got there, he was gone.

I said a few words at my dad's funeral. They were things that I had been thinking about during his last days in the hospital as well as thoughts that I had wrestled with for years.

"We all know that Dad had his rough days," I said. "But there's something else that I know: when he had good days, he taught me how to love a wife. On his good days, he protected my mother, he took care of my mother, he loved my mother, and nobody was going to mess with her."

I didn't feel too much emotion when my dad died. But I do remember one thought going through my head, and it was something difficult for me to accept.

I will never be able to have the kind of relationship with my father that a son should have because now he's dead.

Driving down the road, I wept about that. I had tried for so many years to make that relationship happen. I saw men my age, friends who had good relationships with their dads. I thought that if I tried hard enough, I could fix things between my dad and I. But I don't know – maybe we had too many things to overcome from my early years. Maybe my dad had too many things locked away, old emotional issues that kept a wall between us.

About a year after my dad died, I still found myself thinking about the relationship I had with him. Or the lack of one. It still upset me from time to time, but then a thought entered my head.

My dad did the best he could with what he had.

He had a fourth grade education. His own father was an alcoholic. His grandfather was an alcoholic. He grew up with all these learned behaviors about how fathers relate with their sons, and, unintentionally, he patterned his own life after them. He treated me the same way he was treated. I think he tried to do the best he could to take care of his family with the resources that he had.

I came to this realization, and I felt okay with it. I moved on. I finished fighting and decided not to let it eat me up anymore.

But I also learned that being a dad doesn't have to mean being the same dad to your kids that your father was to you. Just because my dad and I didn't have the kind of relationship I wanted to have, it doesn't mean that I can't have that with my sons.

One of the proudest moments in my life came when I looked at my oldest son on his wedding day in 2004. Fi and I never had any problems with our boys, something that probably made their moving out of the house more difficult than if they had been rebels like I had been.

I looked at him standing there in his tux, and I thought back through all that had happened since the day he was born. That moment in time, when he came screaming out into the world, ended up being the beginning of some of the best times in my life. The days of our recovery.

"Greg, how did you get to be this age?" I asked him. "Yesterday you were just a baby."

I felt the presence of God at their wedding in an amazing way. I saw how happy he and his wife looked, the way they stared into each other's eyes with absolute joy and devotion, and I had some flashbacks. If you looked at pictures of Fi during our wedding day, you would see the sadness in her eyes. With the benefit of hindsight I now know about all the pain locked inside of her: she was mourning the loss of Angie, she was depressed, she had a pastor already harassing her emotionally, and she had gone through sexual abuse as a child, something she didn't even consciously remember.

When I thought about that, I couldn't help but wonder.

"If only —"

If only we would have gotten some counseling.

If only someone would have said, "Hey, guys, just wait. Think about this. Let's work through the problems you have first."

If only someone would have stepped into Fi's life when she was younger and helped her work through her pain and her anger.

For years, Fi couldn't even remember our wedding anniversary — she thought we got married on the 3rd, when we actually got married on the 29th. It just didn't mean that much to her, apart from being one of the saddest days of her life.

117

My son's wedding brought back a lot of memories along with some regret. I thought it would have been so special to have the same relationship with Fi that my son had with his wife on their wedding day. You could tell that they were so into each other.

I also thought about their future. I considered the unknowns, the things that life might throw at them, the ways they would hurt each other and love each other and build each other up.

Man, I hope he doesn't ever have to go through what we did. I hope he never has to feel that kind of pain.

But I also hope that he finds the kind of lasting love that Fi and I have found. The kind of love that's stronger than anything else on earth.

Chapter Seventeen
And Then We Danced

Mike

In the late nineties, when I was still a pastor down in West Chester, I officiated a wedding for some friends of ours. It was a beautiful ceremony, and afterwards, Fi and I went to the reception together and sat at our table. I had performed so many weddings by that time that they no longer reminded me of my own wedding day. But there's still something so special about weddings, and I was glad to be there with Fi.

They did the typical stuff: the father of the bride dancing with the bride, which of course brings everyone to the verge of tears. Then the first dance for the newly married couple: they moved together around the floor, close to one another, whispering to each other.

Dancing is such an intimate thing: two people standing toe to toe, face to face, holding each other close. They are completely in each other's space, but it

119

works because they move as one, they step together, and they do not resist each other. It's such a beautiful metaphor for a marriage relationship.

I don't know what came over Fi, but when everyone else got up to go dance, she grabbed my arm.

"Come on," she said, smiling. "Let's go dance."

I wasn't sure. Dancing was so foreign to me – when I got saved in the 60s, dancing was seen as the sole property of the devil. If you decided to follow Jesus and go to church, you certainly didn't dance. Add to that the fact that I was licensed by a denomination that, at the time, didn't look too fondly on dancing, and I felt reluctant.

"Come on!" Fi said again, and if you know her, you know exactly how her voice sounded in that moment: she was daring me to do it, the same way she had dared her brothers to do things when she was a kid.

I dug my heels in.

"I don't think so," I said.

So we sat there, watching the other couples dance, watching them move gracefully together around the floor.

It's interesting – when I think of dancing, I think of movement. Moving through life. When I think of dancing through life as a married couple, I think there are a lot of ways to look at that.

There are times when, as a couple, you begin dancing together. When you meet and start dating and then get married, you are like a couple who has only just begun dancing for the first time: sometimes the steps are awkward because you don't know each other very well. Perhaps you bump up against each other clumsily, or you have to pause and get your footing again. Maybe you're not sure where to put your hands, or how much pressure to exert, or how fast to turn.

But as you dance together more often, the dance becomes easier, so long as you are paying attention to one another and learning more about how the other person moves. You start to enjoy the movement – then you don't even have to think about it anymore. Soon you are moving around the dance floor, oblivious to the other couples. You hold conversations, whisper to each other, or even close your eyes.

You just keep dancing.

But a relationship is like dancing in other ways.

You might reach a point where you get tired of dancing. Maybe you just don't feel like it anymore. Perhaps you both walk off the dance floor and take a break, still sitting beside each other, still holding hands, but no longer moving together in that intimate way. There are seasons to life, just as there are seasons to relationships.

Often during my marriage, and especially during those first five years, I didn't think I would ever dance with Fi – not on a dance floor and certainly not in life. Nothing came easy to us. We usually seemed to be at crossed purposes, one of us heading this way, the other heading that way. There was no intimacy to keep us close and moving together.

But then life began to change. My friends prayed for Fi. God spoke to me. Metaphorically speaking, we got up from the table and walked on to the dance floor. Like people learning to dance for the first time, we were awkward, we stepped on each other's toes, but we were trying. We were communicating. Our marriage began to dance.

I remember walking the streets of Nashville with Fi in 1998. Her entire extended family was there – we had taken a charter bus down from Lancaster – and we formed a rather unruly mob. Her mom was there along with Fi's seven brothers and sisters and their husbands and wives, and all twenty-some grandkids (plus maybe even a great-grandchild or two).

The city expanded in front of us, full of endless possibilities. We walked down 2nd Avenue North and arrived at the Wild Horse Saloon, a large, three-story brick building with yellow columns holding up a small roof that covered the sidewalk. It was one of our destinations that day, and all forty of us piled inside, laughing and talking and happy to be out of the bus.

Inside we took a walk around – beautiful wood floors stretched through that old saloon, and the dance floor had a vaulted ceiling right up to the roof with the second-floor balcony looking down on it. The ornate decorations and cool atmosphere impressed me.

They turned on the music, and a bunch of people started line dancing – it was a lot of fun watching the nieces and nephews (and some of the aunts and uncles) strutting their stuff. We all had fun and shouted back and forth and cheered at the end of each song. Everyone on the dance floor tried to persuade those who were seated to join them.

I wasn't planning on dancing.

Then the lights went down low, and a slow-dance started. Some couples made their way out on to the shiny floor. They drew close to each other and danced. Standing off in the shadows, everyone else watched them as they made their way together.

I felt Fi's hand reach over for mine. We looked at each other.

"Should we?" her eyes seemed to ask me.

I had to smile. I could tell she wasn't going to push me, but I could also tell that she really wanted to dance, so I nodded, and we both stood up.

I felt extremely self-conscious as we walked out amongst the dancers, and I tried to hide us somewhere in the middle. But the lights were low, and suddenly it just didn't matter what anyone else thought. I put my arm around Fi's waist, and with my other arm, I lifted up her hand. She looked into my eyes with one of the happiest smiles I've ever seen.

We started moving together, a little hesitant at first. It took us a moment to discover each other's rhythm, to move together. We had never danced before, ever, so there were a few bumps and a few squashed toes. But soon we talked quietly, leaning into each other, gliding slowly around the floor. Our hands began to feel comfortable in their place, the pressure just right.

And then we danced.

PRACTICAL APPLICATION

Chapter One
Get to Know Your Spouse Better

Mike

A big realization hit me in the early 90s when we took the Meyer's-Briggs personality profile test. It's a series of questions designed to help you assess your personality type.

What Fi and I learned was that we are about as opposite as two people can possibly be. In every single area, we are at different ends of the spectrum.

One of the ways that this impacts our marriage on a daily basis is with our communication. I often heard her exclaim (with some disgust), "You never told me that!" even though I knew for a fact that I had. She was upset, feeling that I never told her anything, and it made me kind of mad to think that she wasn't listening to me.

Turns out our personality types had a lot to do with this miscommunication: my personality type leads me to review things over and over again in my mind without actually voicing the issue. In fact, some people with my profile will think about something so much that they'll begin to believe that they've spoken about it, *even when they haven't told anyone.*

"Hon, I know I told you that!" I'd say.

"There's no way you told me that," she'd reply. "I've never heard that before in my life."

There I was, learning that it's quite possible, even probable, that all these years I was thinking that I had told Fi things that I hadn't and then getting upset with her when she got upset with me for not telling her.

Something else that our personality profiles brought to the forefront was the difference in the amount of emotion that we experience. Fi, for many reasons, does not experience emotions the way most people do – her emotions come to her through a fog and rarely move her. My emotions, on the other hand, are overly active.

One specific area that this has impacted our marriage is in the romantic element. This area has suffered over the years because while there is a part of romance that occurs in the brain, if it doesn't touch your heart then it's very limited. If romance doesn't become emotional in some sense, then it doesn't happen.

Couples need to become students of each other. That's one thing I did with Fi, and this is something I tell everyone that I counsel: "I made up my mind to become a student of my wife. I wanted to know her better than I know myself. I wanted to know why she was in the kind of mood she was in, why did she look at me that way, why wouldn't she look at me or talk to me. As I did this, I started to understand her love language.

125

I started to read her better than I ever had before. I'd get home from work, and she'd have that look on her face, and I knew one of the boys had been up to no good. Or she'd have a different look on her face, and I knew that I was in trouble. Or I knew that she was in a great mood.

1) Think back over your life. What are its defining moments? You can list a few of them here:

_____

_____

_____

_____

_____

_____

_____

2) Have you ever discussed these moments with your husband or wife? Why or why not?

_____

_____

_____

_____

_____

3) How have these events affected your relationships?

_____

_____

_____

_____

_____

_____

4) What are you doing with the anger that you feel regarding these incidents?

_____
_____
_____
_____
_____
_____
_____
_____

Action Item – Open up your lines of communication. Talk about one thing that you do not normally bring up with your spouse.

Chapter Two
Open Up Your Emotions

Fi

My lack of memories continues to affect me. I wish I could remember being abused when I was four because I think that in some way it might help me experience emotion and work through it. I wish I could figure out how to get angry at the man and others who hurt me instead of only getting angry at the people that I love.

But for some reason I still, after all these years, won't let myself go there. I want to remain in control of my emotions, and when I go there, I can feel myself losing control of my surroundings

If there's anything I want to communicate to you, it's that you cannot get to the place where you are constantly shutting down your emotions! Stay alive! Let yourself experience life: the pain and the pleasure, the ugliness and the beauty. If you start shutting down, it will ruin the rest of your life and steal any joy you may have experienced. Shutting down could ruin existing relationships that you have.

1) What was the family dynamic in which you grew up?

_____

_____

_____

_____

_____

_____

2) Share a memory about a time when you felt emotionally hurt as a child:

_____

_____

_____

_____

_____

_____

3) Share a memory about a time when you felt your happiest as a child:

_____

_____

_____

_____

4) Do you have a desire to have a good relationship with your parents?

_____

_____

_____

_____

5) What would be some ways that you could begin to explore those relationships again?

_____
_____
_____
_____
_____
_____
_____

Action Item – Consider reviewing your answers to these questions with your spouse or counselor.

Chapter Three
The Impact of Money

Mike

The main instigator of problems in most marriage relationships has to do with money: how we spend it, save it, use it, and abuse it. Each individual has their own way of looking at money, so it's no wonder that when two individuals agree to spend the rest of their life together, money often causes conflict and misunderstanding.

One of the best things you can do as a couple is get to the place where your love for each other is so strong that it will not be affected by the amount of money that you have. Answer these questions and think more about your view of money.

1) What was your economic situation growing up?

_____

_____

_____

_____

_____

_____

_____

2) How did you view work and money while you were growing up?

_____

_____

_____

_____

_____

_____

_____

3) How do you think the economic situation you grew up in affects the way you view money today?

_____

_____

_____

_____

_____

_____

_____

Action Item – Set some financials goals with your spouse. Write them down, and then list the steps it would take to reach those goals.

Chapter Four
Trust – Let Your Guard Down

Fi

Mike is a very romantic guy, and I think that through the years I've gotten better at receiving this from him than I was years ago. I now understand that his romance is not always going to lead me to the bedroom. If you've been impacted by a sexual predator, then you know how everything that person does, no matter how kind and well-meaning it might appear on the surface, is designed to get you into bed. After years of being in a relationship like that, it took me quite some time to realize that often Mike just wants to do nice things for me in order to make me happy, to see me smile.

Because of my past, I have to constantly remind myself to put my guard down.

1) Who were your main influencers when you were young?

_____
_____
_____
_____
_____
_____
_____

2) Did the people around you during your childhood give you confidence or speak negative messages into your life? Do you remember any specific instances of this?

_____
_____
_____
_____
_____
_____
_____

3) What scared you as a child? What gave you comfort and made you feel at peace?

_____
_____
_____
_____
_____
_____
_____

4) Where is your self-confidence level right now? How do you feel about you, right now?

_____
_____
_____
_____
_____
_____
_____

Action Item – Figure out one thing that helps to raise your self-confidence (having quiet time, going for a walk, reading a particular verse in the Bible, engaging in activities with your spouse, etc). Make a commitment to doing that thing once a day or once a week.

Chapter Five
The Presence of Pain

Mike

Emotional pain is something we all experience. It's so important to realize what is causing our emotional pain and then discover steps we can take to work through it.

1) Did you have any sort of religious upbringing? Do you see that as a positive or a negative influence in your life?

    _____
    _____
    _____
    _____
    _____
    _____

2) Did you experience any abuse (physical, sexual, emotional) as a child? If so, how has that affected you?

_____

_____

_____

_____

_____

_____

3) Do you consider yourself to be someone who is in touch with your emotions, or do you often feel detached from what is going on around you?

_____

_____

_____

_____

_____

_____

4) If you've answered yes to some of these questions, how have you dealt with the accompanying pain?

_____

_____

_____

_____

_____

_____

Action Item – Once again, find a safe person to talk to about your emotional pain and begin addressing the causes.

Chapter Six
Secrets

Fi

Think about when you were young and you had a secret: who did you tell? Usually children tell secrets to their best friends, and they keep secrets from adults because they're scared that if the adult finds out, they'll get into trouble.

Now consider your spouse in light of this example. Are you keeping secrets from your spouse?

1) Describe the first time you saw your spouse:

_____

_____

_____

_____

_____

2) What drew you to him or her?

_____
_____
_____
_____
_____
_____

3) Are there any secrets that you have kept from your spouse? What would be an appropriate way to bring these secrets to light?

_____
_____
_____
_____
_____
_____

4) What are you and your spouse doing to become best friends?

_____
_____
_____
_____
_____
_____

Action Item – Prayerfully consider sharing your secrets.

Chapter Seven
Enjoy Doing Something Together

Mike

Find something recreational that you can do together. Figure out one or two things that you both enjoy doing, that you both have fun doing, and then, do that together. When you do this, you both see each other at your happiest moments, loving life. Isn't that what you saw when you dated? Isn't that what drew the two of you together: having fun and laughing and seeing the other person having a good time?

In your dating years, you saw the best of that girl or that guy, and that's what you fell in love with. If you make time for recreational activities, you will start to see those things again, and you will start to fall in love again.

Fi and I love riding motorcycles. When we stop at a red light and I look over at her, she is grinning and having a blast. She loves it, I love it, and it reminds me of the girl that I fell in love with. We love watching sports together and going to see live productions such as plays and musicals.

Make time for fun. It could resurrect your marriage.

1) How did you and your spouse spend time together when you were still dating, before you got married?

_____

_____

_____

_____

_____

_____

_____

2) Were there any major events that happened early on in your marriage that shaped what your relationship would look like in the coming years?

_____

_____

_____

_____

_____

_____

_____

3) How do you deal with pain and loss? How do you and your spouse talk about these things?

_____

_____

_____

_____

_____

_____

4) If you have been through a tragedy and are still engaged, have you considered postponing the wedding until you have the opportunity to grieve?

_____

_____

_____

_____

_____

_____

5) If you have been through a tragedy while married, patience is the key. How could you take some time and get the help that you need to work through this tragedy?

_____

_____

_____

_____

_____

_____

Action Item – Schedule a time for you and your spouse to have fun doing something you both enjoy. Get it on your calendar now!

Chapter Eight
Priorities

Mike

There are many good things we can get involved with in our lives. There are youth groups and young adult groups. There's church. We can receive more education. We involve our children in activities.

Yet, many times the busy-ness of life pushes our marriage to the back burner. This can be the first step down a road you do not want to travel.

Answer these questions, and think about where your marriage ranks among the other parts of your life.

    1) How do you feel about your spouse? List the things you truly love about them.

           _____
           _____
           _____
           _____

2) What is the most painful experience you and
   your spouse have gone through together? Did it
   draw you closer together or push you apart?

   _____
   _____
   _____
   _____
   _____

3) What life events have changed your
   relationship?

   _____
   _____
   _____
   _____
   _____

4) Honestly look at your relationship and your life:
   what things are taking precedence over your
   marriage?

   _____
   _____
   _____
   _____
   _____

Action Item – This week do one thing that helps your
spouse to see that your marriage is more important
than anything else.

Chapter Nine
Selfishness

Mike

The true measure of a successful marriage is the ability to which you are able to serve the other person. Period. If a marriage consists of two people working their absolute hardest to serve the other, there is no room or reason for selfishness.

Yet, we are all individuals, and we will battle with selfishness every day. Our sexual relationship with our spouse is just one area where selfishness can become apparent. Think through these questions and be mindful of how selfish (or not) your first responses might be.

1) How has your premarital view, or premarital experience of sex, affected sex in your marriage?

_____

_____

_____

_____

_____

_____

2) List the things that you know the Bible says about sex?

_____

_____

_____

_____

_____

_____

3) How sensitive are you to your spouse's sexual needs?

_____

_____

_____

_____

_____

_____

Action Item – Make a list of things your spouse has recently required of you. How was your attitude when it came to fulfilling these requests? How could you go even further in serving your spouse than simply doing what they've asked?

146

Chapter Ten
Going Back to Fun

Mike

When we first got married, I wanted to be with Fi, and I didn't want her being with other people. When she wanted to go out with her friends at night, I often thought to myself, *This isn't how it ought to be.* I was always at home at night, and I wanted her to be home with me.

Through the years, I learned that's just not how life is. I discovered that my wife needs other people! Can you believe that? She needs to spend time with her friends and her sisters, and she needs to go out and have a good time.

So instead of me pouting and giving her a hard time about leaving, I made a change: I started asking her for two things. I ask her to make sure that she laughs a lot and has fun.

There's one thing that I've learned – if I gave her that freedom, our relationship was better. She actually treated me better.

1) Do the things that you say to your spouse build them up or tear them down?

_____
_____
_____
_____
_____
_____

2) When do you spend the most time laughing with your spouse?

_____
_____
_____
_____
_____

3) What were the things that made you laugh when you first met?

_____
_____
_____
_____

Action Item – List three activities you could do with your spouse that would involve laughter. Now go and schedule one of those.

Chapter Eleven
The Work You Have to Do

Fi

I want so bad for you to know that you don't have to give up. Your marriage is worth fighting for! If I can do it, if Mike and I could make it through the stuff we encountered, then you can make it, too. You're going to pay the price for your relationships sooner or later. You can pay that price now and work through things with your spouse, or you can put off payment and split up. But some day, maybe in your next relationship, you will have to work through those issues.

I'd rather keep working hard, keep trying to find my emotions and myself, right here with the kids and man that God gave me. My husband loves me and honors me. I'm not going to get that anywhere else.

Sometime around the year 2000, I had an encounter with grace. A friend of mine just kept talking about grace – the topic seemed to come up in all of our conversations.

"Well, what is grace?" I asked.

A pastor's wife asking for a definition of grace!

She explained it to me. Then, one morning I sat in the kitchen having quiet time, and suddenly I saw it. I just saw it: God's grace. It was a beautiful, overwhelming moment.

1) Think of three ways you can unconditionally love or respect your spouse:

_____

_____

_____

_____

_____

_____

2) Who do you spend most of your time with? Do these relationships help or hurt your marriage?

_____

_____

_____

_____

_____

3) Are there any problems in your relationship that you are running away from?

_____

_____

_____

_____

_____

Action Item – Think about the term "grace." What does it mean to you? Do you have an accurate definition of the word? Talk with your spouse about what grace means to them.

Chapter Twelve
Take Out the Trash

Mike

Our friend Tommy Wilson often rode his motorcycle with Fi and I. He had a trailer with a special cover. He tried to fix that thing one day, smiling and happy, and when he realized there was nothing more that he could do with it, he turned to me and said something interesting.

In a play on words, what he said just happened to contain the last name of our old pastor, the one who had caused such havoc in our lives. I felt this surge of anger rise up inside of me, the same feelings I always felt when someone said that man's name.

"I don't want anything to do with that name," I practically spat at him.

He looked at me with consternation in his eyes and said something that at first made me so mad I wanted to punch him.

151

"Mike," he said without backing down. "You need to take out the trash."

Who does Tommy think he is? I thought to myself. *He didn't go through what I went through. He doesn't have the right to tell me to take out the trash — he doesn't know how I feel.*

He had preached a message prior to that about taking out the trash — it was about all the crud that builds up in our mind and how at some point you have to just put it on the curb and let the trash man get rid of it, haul it off.

You need to take out the trash.

His words reverberated in my mind. I wanted to stay mad at him, but I couldn't. This was a man who had loved my wife and I in spite of our story, in spite of the things we had been through. He had loved us to the point that we could love God again. I knew he cared deeply for Fi and I.

I do have to take out the trash, I thought to myself.

When I decided to take out the trash, it helped my marriage relationship in an incredible way. I found more time and emotional energy to devote to the happiness of my wife and the betterment of our marriage. After I took out the trash, our marriage was like a clean house.

1) What are the things you like most about your marriage?

_____

_____

_____

_____

_____

_____

_____

2) What are the things you would like to improve in your marriage?

_____
_____
_____
_____
_____
_____
_____

3) Is there someone that you need to consider forgiving? Write their name(s) down here, even if you're not ready to forgive them just yet:

_____
_____
_____
_____
_____
_____
_____

Action Item – When is the last time you prayed about your marriage? Take a moment now and pray about question #2.

Chapter Thirteen
Agree to Disagree

Mike

One of the things that separated us for some time had to do with cleaning. My wife is a perfectionist when it comes to cleaning (and after reading her story, you can understand why). I am no slob, but I'm also not a perfectionist.

When we first moved to West Chester and started our church, she worked at a market on Fridays, so on Friday night, it was just our two boys and I. When Fi wasn't home, we made a mess and had a blast. I cleaned up the boys, put them in bed, and tidied up the house before she got home. At the end of the night, I vacuumed the basement and put everything away.

The minute she came home, she redid everything. She grabbed the vacuum and went over every area that I had just vacuumed! Not only that, but I could tell she was angry that she even had to do it. That didn't make for a very pleasant evening or for a pleasant week.

I could never clean well enough for her. That's something I felt a lot in our marriage relationship: the things that I did were not good enough for her. Although I don't think I was conscious of it at the time, I'm sure that echoing in the back of my mind were my father's words: "You'll never amount to anything." Her cleaning after me made me so mad one night, and she could tell that I was upset.

At some point, we talked about this and came to a healthy conclusion: we were different in a lot of areas. We needed to accept the fact that, most likely, we would remain different in these areas for the rest of our lives. A deal was struck – when it came to this sort of thing, and especially when it came to cleaning, we agreed to disagree and not be upset at each other.

We took that a step further and began to analyze different areas of our relationship, identifying places that this mindset might help our relationship grow stronger. We had grown up in two totally different cultures, with different parents and family values. It was inevitable that we would disagree about certain things.

I'll tell you: that was the greatest thing that Fi and I ever did for each other. She used to get angry at me because I wasn't cleaning up to her perfect standards, and I got ticked at her because I worked hard trying to make the house look nice, so she didn't have to clean, only for her to come home and redo everything. Then we agreed to disagree, and it was a turning point, the start to a marriage that felt totally different.

The Bible says that it's the little fox that spoils the vine. It's the little bitty things in your marriage relationship that kill, and if you can't agree to disagree on some of these little things, you will always be angry and upset and miss out on enjoying your spouse. You'll never have the peace and happiness you need in your marriage relationship.

155

1) Have you thought about connecting with a couple that has a strong marriage? Who are some couples that you know and respect?

_____

_____

_____

_____

_____

_____

_____

Action Item – Talk to your spouse about some areas where you can agree to disagree.

Chapter Fourteen
Different Expectations

Mike

I thought all marriages were the way my mom and dad's marriage was. My mom didn't have a license, so she never went anywhere without my dad. When dad went away, most of the time mom went with him. It was a huge revelation to me at some point in my relationship with Fi when I realized, *That is not how most marriages are.*

When I finally realized that, it helped me to back off and give Fi more freedom. Giving her more freedom helped our relationship. But I still asked for two things:

"Call me when you get there," I said. "And call me when you leave. I just want to make sure that you're okay."

But for a long time, she thought that was an attempt to control her. When she realized that all I wanted to do was protect her and know she was safe, it made a huge difference in how we treated each other.

157

1) What are your expectations of marriage?

_____

_____

_____

_____

_____

_____

2) What are some things that you could do to help fulfill your spouse's expectations of marriage?

_____

_____

_____

_____

_____

3) What could you do to help your spouse achieve their purpose in life?

_____

_____

_____

_____

4) Are you allowing past hurts to keep you from doing what you know you ought to be doing? What would be some steps to getting back on the right track?

_____

_____

_____

_____

_____

5) When was the last time you heard from God about the call He has on your life?

_____

_____

_____

_____

_____

_____

_____

Action Item – Consider reading *The Purpose Driven Life* in order to gain a better understanding of the reason for your existence.

Chapter Fifteen
Anger

Fi

There are many indicators that will come up in your life, clueing you in to areas of pain. For me, the presence of anger began to let me know that something wasn't quite right. Something in my past still had a hold on me.

You cannot stuff your feelings and be healthy. You may not be able to unpack these feelings until you speak with a professional counselor.

1) How do you deal with anger? When is the last time you were angry?

   _____

   _____

   _____

   _____

2) What is something that makes you feel angry or frustrated on a regular basis?

_____

_____

_____

_____

_____

_____

_____

3) Are you willing to share your feelings with a professional counselor? If not, what's holding you back?

_____

_____

_____

_____

_____

_____

_____

Action Items – If you have issues with anger surrounding unresolved events or relationships from your past, call a counselor today and set up an appointment.

Chapter Sixteen
Never Give Up

Fi

Sometimes people ask me, "How were you able to remain married after all that you went through?"

"Blood, sweat and tears," I tell them.

Some of the time, it was sheer will power and determination. I knew in my heart that my marriage was something worth fighting for...most days. Of course there were some days (I think that if we're honest, we'll all admit to having them) when I didn't care. But most of the time I feel committed and decisive, that this marriage is what I want and it's worth fighting for.

I was also highly influenced by my upbringing – you learn in the Amish community that divorce is not an option, so you might as well work it out. Our culture played a huge role in keeping us together.

Personal counseling also helped me a lot.

1) How did your father treat your mother?

_____
_____
_____
_____
_____
_____

2) How did your mother treat your father?

_____
_____
_____
_____
_____
_____

3) Do you want to treat your spouse the way your parents treated each other? If so, why? If not, why not?

_____
_____
_____
_____
_____
_____

Action Item – Ask your spouse to describe the relationship their parents had and whether or not that is the kind of marriage they would also like to have.

Chapter Seventeen
Love Languages

Mike

If I only had thirty minutes and I was with a couple who was really struggling or even with a couple who just wanted to improve their marriage, this is what I would do: I would help them to discover their primary love language. When a couple is in trouble, it is because both of their love tanks are absolutely empty.

I would go through the five love languages and help them to discover what they are. Then, they have to learn to fill each other's love tanks. That's one of the best tools that I use as a counselor.

Fi's love language is Acts of Service. The way I discovered that is by how much importance she puts on me taking care of the things she asks me to do. When I do those things, she is a happy camper, like at no other time. I can give her flowers, but that doesn't make her as happy as she gets when I do things for her around the house. I can spend time with her. We do all of those things. But nothing means quite so much to her as when I do things for her.

So I take a cup of coffee to her every single morning. I get up early, make her coffee exactly how she likes it, and I take it to her. She loves that.

1) What kind of dance are you doing in your marriage?

_____

_____

_____

_____

2) Is that dance one that is moving you and your spouse forward, or is that dance one where you are constantly stepping on each other's toes?

_____

_____

_____

_____

3) How could you better move together in the dance of life?

_____

_____

_____

_____

4) When is the last time you spent time with your spouse and just didn't want it to end?

_____

_____

_____

_____

Action Item – Consider reading the book *The Five Love Languages* with your spouse and make a commitment to filling their love tank.

Special thanks to...

Shawn Smucker for his support, encouragement, patience, and his incredible talent. We couldn't have written this book without you.

Jonas and Anne Beiler, for encouraging us to tell our story.

Gentry Austin, for using his unique gifts to help us design the cover of this book

Meghan Glick and Kristin Staley, for reading an early draft and giving us your feedback.

Andi Cumbo, for editing this book in such a loving way.

Our Heavenly Father, because without his healing in our lives and our marriage, we would never have been able to dance.

About the Authors

Mike and Fi Lusby have been married for 36 years.

Mike is a certified Life and Health Coach, helping people go from normalcy to excellence. He is also a public speaker conducting workshops on health and marriage and has been a licensed minister with the Assemblies of God for 30 years.

Fi works for the Beiler Family Office as a travel assistant for her sister, Anne Beiler. She is a singing artist and works with a ministry encouraging women to share their stories.

Mike and Fi have two sons, a daughter-in-love, and a grandson. They currently reside in Gap, PA.

To arrange a speaking engagement, book signing, or any other event with Mike and Fi, please contact them at filusby@gmail.com

Shawn Smucker lives in Paradise, Pennsylvania with his wife Maile and their four children. He is a co-writer, author, and he blogs daily at shawnsmucker.com

If you are interested in having him help you write your own story, contact him at shawnsmucker@yahoo.com

This is his fifth book.